Spoiler Alert

Forerunners: Ideas First

Short books of thought-in-process scholarship, where intense analysis, questioning, and speculation take the lead

FROM THE UNIVERSITY OF MINNESOTA PRESS

(Continued on page 87)

Spoiler Alert
A Critical Guide

Aaron Jaffe

University of Minnesota Press

MINNEAPOLIS

LONDON

Portions of this book were published in "There Is as Yet Insufficient Data for a Meaningful Answer: Information at the Literary Limit," *The Year's Work in the Oddball Archive,* ed. Jonathan Eburne and Judith Roof (Bloomington: Indiana University Press, 2016); "Pop Culture," *The Bloomsbury Handbook of Literary and Cultural Theory,* ed. Jeffrey R. Di Leo (London: Bloomsbury Academic, 2018); and "Updating as Modernity; or, Impermanent Test Dept.," *Thresholds,* http://openthresholds.org/.

Published by the University of Minnesota Press
111 Third Avenue South, Suite 290
Minneapolis, MN 55401–2520
http://www.upress.umn.edu

Available as a Manifold edition at manifold.umn.edu

The University of Minnesota is an equal-opportunity educator and employer.

I give you the mausoleum of all hope and desire; it's rather excruciatingly apt that you will use it to gain the reducto absurdum of all human experience which can fit your individual needs no better than it fitted his or his father's. I give it to you not that you may remember time, but that you might forget it now and then for a moment and not spend all your breath trying to conquer it.

—WILLIAM FAULKNER, *The Sound and the Fury*

Spoiler Alert for those who have not read the book: William Dorrit was never able to escape the influence of 23 years in the Marshalsea, and on the evening of his death in Venice he imagined he was back in prison again. Of his children, only Amy remained humble and true to herself throughout the journey.

—JANEAUSTENSWORLD.WORDPRESS.COM

Contents

Spoiler Alert

CONTENT WARNING: During this book, we will be discussing a variety of content subjects that may induce memoplexy. If you have any reservations, for whatever reason, about reading, watching, hearing, or discussing certain types of content, please consult a professional.

Introduction: Spoilers Ahead

ISHMAEL, buoyant on Queequeg's coffin.

Mrs. Ramsey won't make it to the lighthouse.

Reader, she married him. Caddy gets away, but a magazine picture found by the county librarian shows her with a Nazi in a car in Paris.

In the mirror Benjy sees nothing. Neither does Jake.

Gatsby is dead, still floating in the deep end. As is Joe Gillis.

Iago did it. *Demand nothing of him: what you know, you know. From this time forth I never will speak.* Hamlet didn't do anything. Eventually, the negative state is important. Everyone else either did it or didn't. Sort of. They may have forgotten. Rosebud is a sled. The Maltese Falcon is fake. Time and tide wait for no man. Neither do blood, chocolate, grass stains, lipstick, beef fat, a gangrenous scratch—all the spoiling things. The pizza is on the roof. The briefcase is the protagonist. So is the photograph in the *Collector's Guide to Plastic Purses*. Godot never arrives, but keep the meeting.

King Kong Theory boils down to "Beauty and/or 30-caliber Vickers twin-mounted machineguns."[1] Reader, Slothrop is still missing in the zone.

"The marvelous thing is that it's painless"—the writer's spoiling words can't be trusted. "That's how you know when it starts."[2] In

---

1. Douglas G. Kenney, "Spoilers!," *National Lampoon,* April 1971, 35. The difference between common knowledge and what's readily knowable is worthy of emphasizing. In an age of total information, paper notation/ citation itself may function as a spoiler alert, even as citations supplement what's readily knowable with a paper trail of bibliographic facts.

2. Ernest Hemingway, *The Snows of Kilimanjaro* (New York: Scribner, 1995), 3.

the beginning was the pun. *The world, which seems to lie before us like a land of dreams, so various, so beautiful, so new, hath really neither joy, nor love, nor light, nor certitude, nor peace, nor help for pain.*

In the end, entropy triumphs. Information, eaten by chatter. Comment sections get more and more toxic, best to avoid them: *lie down where all the ladders start in the foul rag and bone shop of the heart. In the destructive element immerse* . . . the spoiling gestures. Reader, the narrator did it, but there's still insufficient information for a meaningful answer.

Old Yeller got rabies.

Cue up the emoji: the celestial parrot descends; Invisible man living on in the grid; Yoda and Chewbacca are old friends. The arc of the galaxy bends toward Vader. *The circle is now complete,* the mausoleum of all hope and desire, well before it is dreamed of; see Reddit. More human than human, a thing arrives from the future thinking it's human. The small baby dies, predeceasing the rest. "Literature has more dogs than babies, and also more abortions. . . . [Other people's babies are] often noted to not be of interest."[3] Dorrit remains perpetually little. Your friends will save you from the Goblin Market. The nurse recognizes Odysseus by his scar. Oedipus solves the riddle. Medea *deserves her revenge, and we deserve to die.* Huck goes to hell. Miss Quinten, too. The hunger artist is lost in the straw. Bartley prefers not to. Tess is raped. 124 is spiteful; so, too, Jean Grey. *Your parents, they fuck you up. They may not mean to, but they do.* A mad woman upstairs in the attic, she's from the Caribbean, runs the Bates Motel.

The original Final Girl now has a daughter and a granddaughter; their basement is fully prepped and weaponized.

Michael tries to get out, but they drag him back in. Walter gets what's coming, Carl gets bit, no one knows about Tony. *Yes, Game*

---

3. Rivka Galchen, *Little Labors* (New York: New Directions, 2016), 34.

of Thrones' Final Season Will Kill Multiple Characters.[4] *There's a small chance an asteroid will smack into Earth in 2135.*[5] On June 25, 2195, a plenary at the university will make some remarks about Gilead at a symposium. *Life, which you look for, you will never find. For when the gods created man, they let death be his share, and life withheld in their own hands.*[6] *In the long run we are all dead. But this long run is a misleading guide to current affairs. In the long run we are all dead. Economists set themselves too easy, too useless a task, if in tempestuous seasons they can only tell us that when the storm is long past, the ocean is flat again.*[7] Enlightenment is Totalitarian. *Cells interlinked within cells interlinked within one stem. And, dreadfully distinct against the dark, a tall white fountain played.*[8]

Past performance is no guarantee of future results.

Now that we've gotten all that out of the way: the thesis, in miniaturized form, is that spoilers resemble triggers. And vice versa. I mean, reductio absurdum, the premature end is already preprogrammed in, the mechanism always ready to go. The trip wire is set.

It isn't narrative. The spoiler is even less than that. It's a switch, a flop, a knee jerk, an impedance mechanism made operational for a connected world charged with specific knowledge sequencing

4. Jason Cohen, "Yes, Game to Thrones' Final Season Will Kill Multiple Characters," *Comic Book Resources,* March 13, 2018, https://www.cbr.com/game-of-thrones-season-8-who-dies.

5. Cleve R. Wootson, "There's a Small Chance an Asteroid Will Smack into Earth in 2135," *Washington Post,* March 19, 2018, https://www.washingtonpost.com/news/speaking-of-science/wp/2018/03/19/theres-a-small-chance-an-asteroid-will-smack-into-earth-in-2135-nasa-is-working-on-a-plan/?utm_term=.d84b264b80c8.

6. *The Epic of Gilgamesh,* https://www.cs.utexas.edu/users/vl/notes/gilgamesh.html.

7. John Maynard Keynes, *The Collected Writings* (Cambridge: Macmillan/St. Martin's, 1971), 4:65.

8. Vladimir Nabokov, *Pale Fire* (New York: Vintage, 1989), 59. Cf. the baseline operational stability test for automatization-authentication in Denis Villeneuve, *Blade Runner 2049* (Columbia, 2017).

problems. The inevitability of information has changed the critical quality of modernity, leaving us with an acute, diexic vertigo,
a technical feeling *here* that, out *there,* no surprises are left. The
background, foregrounding itself. Take the famous story of Alfred
Hitchcock's *Psycho.* Hitchcock didn't want audiences to spoil it—
namely, the reveal that dutiful psychopath and taxidermied mother are one and the same, spoil it for everyone else, that is, for the
uninitiated to follow. Theater lobbies were filled with cautionary
placards.[9] The Spoiler Alert encloses a world—a *Weltanschauung,*
really—supersaturated with tacit, nondisclosure agreements, le-
gally meaningless pseudo-contracts about hidden knowledge—we
simultaneously didn't agree to and acutely experience as betrayals
of virtuous stupidities.

All this information at our fingertips—in your hands already, in
fact—you might not need to heed any of it. Just sit inertly at your
desk like the guy in that Melville story, Googling nothing. A simple
machine in which output seems programmed, everyone agrees in
advance that the affective-aesthetic access to input today is unprecedented. *Why does it stress us out so much?* Music, for instance:
"Listening to music on streaming platforms ultimately reminds
us that there are lifetimes upon lifetimes of recorded sound that
we won't live long enough to hear."[10] Nothing is spared anymore.
Everything spoils everything now. When there is no longer room
for the Nothing, even the Nothing is spoiled, in so many words.

9. Joan Hawkins, *Cutting Edge: Art-Horror and the Horrific Avant-
Garde* (Minneapolis: University of Minnesota Press, 2000), 77; see Seth
Friedman, "Misdirection in Fits and Starts: Alfred Hitchcock's Popular
Reputation and the Reception of His Films," *Quarterly Review of Film and
Video* 29, no. 1 (2012): 91–93. Cf. Kenney, "The Movie's Multiple Murders
Are Committed by Anthony Perkins Disguised as His Long Dead Mother,"
"Spoilers!," 33.

10. Chris Richards, "Our Access to Music Is Unprecedented,"
Washington Post, March 9, 2018, https://www.washingtonpost.com/lifestyle
/style/our-access-to-music-is-unprecedented-why-does-it-stress-us-out-so
-much/2018/03/07/a00686e6-174a-11e8-b681-2d4d462a1921_story.html.

This regime of compulsory stupidity isn't new; it's hardwired. Spoilers and triggers have secret affinities. One of the first recorded instances of the actual phrase "Spoiler Alert," from a parody feature in *National Lampoon* in 1971, confirms a shared provenance in insurance:

> In more tranquil times, Americans loving nothing better than curling up with a blood-chilling whodunit or trooping off to the cinema to feast on spine-tingling thrillers, weird science fiction tales and hair-raising war adventure. Nowadays, however, with the country a seething caldron of racial, political and moral conflict, the average American has more excitement in his daily life than he can healthily handle. [A]s a public service, [this warning presents] a selection of "spoilers" guaranteed to reduce the risk of unsettling and possibly dangerous suspense. We ask that you read this over several times and, if possible, commit them to memory before you venture into the actual book or late night movie. Remember, the life you save may be your own.[11]

"My old woman is a flea bag and yours is a stinking polecat," but, to spoil the Flannery O'Connor story in question, this man is not a Misfit.[12] There are others.

Culture—the sine qua non of literary humanism—may be, after all, little more than an elaborate cover story for the far more pervasive disposition to stay oblivious as long as possible.[13] An unsolicited package shows up outside the apartment of a husband and wife in Richard Matheson's story "Button, Button" ("The letter was in plain view the whole time"[14]).[15] Inside the package, they find a mysterious gadget, a push-button fastened to wooden box covered by a small, glass dome. Later that day, the scheme is explained: "If you

11. Kenney, "Spoilers!," 33.

12. Flannery O'Connor, "The Life You Save May Be Your Own," in *Collected Works* (New York: Library of America, 1988), 183.

13. Here I'm thinking of Matthijs van Boxsel, *The Encyclopedia of Stupidity* (London: Reaktion, 2005).

14. Kenney, "Spoilers!," 35.

15. Richard Matheson, "Button, Button," in *The Best of Richard Matheson*, 129–37 (New York: Penguin, 2017).

push the button . . . somewhere in the world someone you don't
know will die. In return for which you will receive a payment of
$50,000." They argue about it. Is it only some sick joke? The mon-
ey could mean "that trip to Europe" they always talked about; that
"cottage on the island"; "a nicer apartment, nicer furniture, nicer
clothes, a car"; the financial means "to finally have a baby." Could
they live themselves if they did it, if doing it meant the death for
"some old Chinese peasant ten thousand miles away?"[16] "Some
diseased native in the Congo?" "A baby boy in Pennsylvania?"
"Some beautiful little girl on the next block?" All the racist moves.
She wants to. He doesn't. Eventually, he leaves the apartment, and,
on a whim, she presses it anyway, and someone is indeed killed.
The victim, in fact, turns out to be (who else?) the husband (someone shoved him on the subway track across town), and she learns
that she is the named beneficiary of his insurance policy. She now
stands to receive the amount of $50,000.

Spoiler: . . .

16. For a discussion of this trope, see Eric Hayot, *The Hypothetical
Mandarin* (Oxford: Oxford University Press, 2009).

. . . no one ever really knows everything!

As omnipotent, mimetic cost/benefit machine that triggers a calculation and executes a command, the button is the ultimate memeplex (meme + complex) of the spoiler-as-surprise, memo-plexy designating as a mechanism of parole-as-control. A spoil-ing meme: your meme sauce is weak. Enter the memeplex. About the word—and its cognates ("memoplectic"—"memoplexy")—Richard Dawkins did much to operationalize the root word *meme* following an analogy with gene—proposing meme (rhymes with cream, he says) as a unit of replication, a self-reproducing cultur-al gene. Calls for a human menome project, culturnomics, Digital Humanics, and so on, operationalize a tendentious analogy for various Big Data deliverables.[17]

What gets sometimes lost is not only that the derivation of *meme* itself comes as a *back*-formation from *mimesis*—mimetic, mimicry, imitation—but also the sense of mimicry as a given life-form de-pendent on mimetic data transmission of/to its environment. The memeplex is another word for what Vilém Flusser would call the technical image.[18] Without forgetting a sense of the operation of mimicry degree zero, it is also worth noting a biopolitical sense from medicine of *mimesis* as the visible manifestation of a hidden pathogen not actually present at all. The point of the suffix *-plex* is less the notion that memes cluster together to reproduce themselves (alibi: memes are the sex organs of trolls) than the sense that *-plex*

17. Richard Dawkins, *The Selfish Gene* (Oxford: Oxford University Press, 1976), 192: "We need a name for the new replicator, a noun which conveys the idea of a unit of cultural transmission, or a unit of imitation. 'Mimeme' comes from a suitable Greek root, but I want a monosyllable that sounds a bit like 'gene.' I hope my classicist friends will forgive me if I abbreviate mimeme to meme. . . . It should be pronounced to rhyme with 'cream.'"

18. Vilém Flusser, *Into the Universe of Technical Images* (Minneapolis: University of Minnesota Press, 2011).

denotes a frayed thread—a frayed mimetic wire, as it were.[19] Seriality condensed into technical images. What we're looking at here is not a flattened version of the base/superstructure model—a sentence freighted with precautionary subordinate clauses. Rather, the suffix illustrates a complex, recursively overdetermined horizon, an exploding schematic drawing of the invisible line connecting subjects and objects, present futures (tipping the planes of abstraction on their edges, as it were). Or, perhaps, we might understand the spoiler memeplex in infrastructural terms as a diagram of ruined mediation, a complex wire sparking on both ends. Its etymology denotes both twisting together and encircling or encompassing, multiple parts entwined into a difficult to separate whole, suggestively raising the problem of asymmetry, in which smaller or larger symmetries may or may not be apparent at different scales.

In *Dialectic of Enlightenment,* Theodor Adorno and Max Horkheimer give us not Oedipus and his eponymous complex but Oedipus the humanist inside the spoiler memeplex, spoiling the eternal recurrence of the same. By solving the riddle of the Sphinx, he ruins not only mythology but also the riddle itself. The humanist spoiler: the trigger is man. How to insure what follows?[20] One example is Ursula K. Le Guin's "Wife's Story" ("My own dear love, turned in the hateful one"). It spoils the standard werewolf fable: your husband, the father of your children, is really a dangerous monster—a wolf that transforms into man.[21] But, surprise: you're not a victim, you're a she-wolf, a member of a salubrious pack; so, you and your rapacious sisters flip the script and destroy *him*!

What walks on hind legs during the daytime, then, is the spoiler itself. Totalizing is one thing, totaling is another, but here's

19. See Susan Blackstone, *The Meme Machine* (Oxford: Oxford University Press, 2000), 19.

20. Theodor Adorno and Max Horkheimer, *Dialectic of Enlightenment* (Stanford, Calif.: Stanford University Press, 2002).

21. Ursula K. Le Guin, "The Wife's Story," in *The Compass Rose,* 327–34 (New York: Perennial, 2005).

what spoils it: the two are twinned, intertwined, coarticulated. Totalizing, as Horkheimer and Adorno put it, is part of the modernity program: "private vices are the anticipatory historiography of public virtues in the totalitarian era." Totaling—in the sense of indemnity from damage—provides a temporal loop hole for criticality in the memeplex. In its conflation of totaling and totality, Erich Auerbach's *Mimesis* might be understood as a contribution to the Ur-theory of memoplectics. Edward Said describes Auerbachian method as a kind of finding aid for its own critical method, "an optic, for seeing and then articulating reality."[22] Concerning the spoiler, it's literally the mechanism for totaling both the magic lantern and camera obscura as one gadget, in the sense of the multimedia *Gesamtkunstwerk* imagined by Friedrich Kittler, rendering something from the outside (from the background of "lived experience"[23]) into the foreground as compressed, inverted fragment:

> on the one hand fully externalized description, uniform illumination, uninterrupted connection, free expression, all events in the foreground, displaying unmistakable meanings, few elements of historical development and of psychological perspective; on the other certain parts brought into high relief, others left obscure, abruptness, suggestive influence of the unexpressed, "background" quality, multiplicity of meanings and the universal-historical claims, development of the concept of the historically becoming, and preoccupation with the problematic.[24]

Sequencing is ruined. Auerbach's discussion of *Gargantua and Pantagruel,* in particular, concerns entering the grotesque, cavernous mouth of the giant, which means entering into a media enclosure. Inside, there are cabbages. Astounded by the enormity of this total world, the narrator notices a peasant diligently planting said cabbages. What are you doing here? the narrator asks.

22. Edward Said, introduction to Erich Auerbach, *Mimesis: The Representation of Reality in Western Literature* (Princeton, N.J.: Princeton University Press, 2003), xiii.
23. Auerbach, *Mimesis*, 7.
24. Auerbach, 23.

Making a living, what else should I do?

For Auerbach, mimesis breaks the brain–blood barrier of fore-grounded creatural life and backgrounded grandiosity of humanism. The spoiler memeplex is a form of *motiveless malignity,* a groundless grievance against a literary-aesthetic affect/effect that seems to throw up on us in the most mundane, inopportune ways possible. Auerbach zooms in on Emma Bovary's spoiled meal, bitterness spilling out on her plate along with revolting chunks of boiled beef:

> It was above all at mealtimes that she could bear it no longer, in that little room on the ground floor, with the smoking stove, the creaking door, the oozing walls, the damp floor-tiles; all the bitterness of life seemed to be served to her on her plate, and, with the steam from the boiled beef, there rose from the depths of her soul other exhalations as it were of disgust. Charles was a slow eater; she would nibble a few hazel-nuts, or else, leaning on her elbow, would amuse herself making marks on the oilcloth with the point of her table-knife.[25]

Nothing happens! It's ruining her life!!!

For Auerbach, reality is precarious, a world filled with stimuli, bite-size castoffs of aesthetic integrity—a scar, a cabbage, a plate of boiled beef—that resequence/reorient a certain experience of reality. The spoiler is a bug that's a feature. When it comes to Virginia Woolf's *To the Lighthouse,* the triggering feature is a brown stocking (Auerbach: "realistic depth is achieved in every individual occurrence, for example the measuring of the stocking"[26]). Hovering over the entire episode is the future fact that Mrs. Ramsey's trip to the lighthouse is never going to happen (she is going to die). Here, not only do we have the spoiling words of tiresome Mr. Ramsey but also a discouraging forecast supplied by an actual, bona-fide expert in future conditions, a meteorologist.

Yet, these spoiling words—the predicted extinctions of language and desire—are not sufficient to ruin the day. (Spoiler: it's not just the weather . . .) What pierces subjective reverie in Woolf is the

25. Auerbach, 482–83.
26. Auerbach, 552.

accelerating effect of a young child sharply told by his mother to be still (as she holds a sock up to his fidgeting leg). Mrs. Ramsey is trying to measure and resize the garment she plans to alter and bring as a gift for the lighthouse keeper's son. What happens next is quite telling for spoilers as such: in an instant, the background suddenly becomes foregrounded. The data—the tacit givens—include discarded objects and refuse of the current occupants becoming inescapably present: not perspective as framed by the window, looking across water to the lighthouse, not the anticipated completion of Lily Briscoe's painting with a flick of the wrist, but the actual ruined futurity manifest in a summer house as currently occupied: "if every door in a house is left perpetually open, and no lockmaker in the whole of Scotland can mend a bolt, things must spoil." Reality is eventually totaled by entropy: "Everything is getting spoiled," because "everything goes to ruin."[27] Or, the reverse, *is getting* becomes *goes to*.

Trigger warnings are also memoplectic. The debate in all its reified totality is a discourse rather than a discussion/dialogue, a series of pseudo-propositions about arresting at the threshold of risky metadata. The metadata are, in somewhat circular fashion, the contents, "subjects frequently identified as triggers" to include "abuse, rape, self-injurious behaviors, eating disorders, drug and alcohol addiction, suicide."[28] These matters of concern are condensed into the smallest visible black box of facticity as presuppositional mimesis. The proleptic verbal prohibition equals danger ahead—a force field of control paradigmatically associated with the kind of captive audiences and required readings of classrooms, or, more broadly, with the total, compulsory connectivity associated with a new human Right to be connected to everything—online. Perversely, the other side of this memeplex is a crypto-libertarian idea of total freedom, a freedom-from-warning, not least, presented as the do-

27. Auerbach, 530.
28. E. Beverly et al., "Students' Perceptions of Trigger Warnings in Medical Education," *Teach Learn Med* 30, no. 1: 5–14.

main of pure kairotic decision as a necessary condition of ruinous adulthood, spoiled enlightenment, and so forth. Why won't humans wake up to feel their existential peril? What is preloaded is human being itself with requisite vulnerabilities—a factory fill, as it were, of harmful aesthetic data about harm. The enviable recourse to the phrase *adult material* indicates not protecting a naive ear or an innocuous eye but indemnifying various repeated sensible and sensory experiences from risk as the ruinous condition of adulthood.

Not surprisingly, perhaps, #spoiler tags are a thing:

```
{{#spoiler:hide=hide_message|spoiler_text}}.[29]
```

Furthermore, algorithms are being researched and developed for eliminating exposure to spoilers in data feeds.[30] The aim isn't simply alerting users to the existence of spoilers per se but filtering them out altogether from a given ego feed. First, determine the channel selected for transmitting spoiling content to a user; second, mark the content presented on a comparison with automatically generated metadata sets associated with the totality of experienced and unexperienced metadata; third, determine that any new requested future content exclude spoiler content based on one or more criteria to include known and unknown spoiler metadata. The entertainment integrity of full episodes—entire seasons, entire social networks—hangs in the balance. For the desired program, requested content equals both the spoiler and the spoiler alert. For the program, there is no functional difference—just as with spoilers and spoiler alerts, so, too, triggers and warnings against them.

Not so much with fires and fire alarms, for instance, but this you probably knew already.

---

29. https://www.mediawiki.org/wiki/Extension:Spoilers.
30. See, e.g., Jordan Boyd-Graber, "Spoiler Alert: Machine Learning Approaches to Detect Social Media Posts with Revelatory Information," https://onlinelibrary.wiley.com/doi/pdf/10.1002/meet.14505001073.

Content Warning

The spoiler doesn't miniaturize the text in the form of a summary—a precis, an abstract, Cliff's Notes—as much as it signals new technical sensitivity to activated sensibilities, alerting readers of spoilers ahead that can be spoiled and withholding from them what they are. "Nonreading is not a badge of shame, but the way of the future"—who now would bother with such statements besides an English professor?[31] The way of the future belongs to . . . plastics, ancient aliens, robotic overlords, DH . . . To this end, there's a certain, apposite technical image ubiquitous online these days. Think of it as something like the Divine Trigger. It gets appended to various professionally sponsored tech think-pieces and prognostications with titles like *Human Intelligence vs. Artificial Intelligence: Who'll Be the Winner? Privacy Tech; Turning STEM to STEAM; Hope in an Age of Technological Enhancement; You too can clone yourself*; and so on.[32]

Computer, find me a "royalty-free" "licensable" version of Michelangelo's *Creation of Adam,* in which Adam himself is a replicant.[33]

What we have in this image is the awkward, physically impossible handshake between the human and the machine. One hand, the right one, extending leftward, is flesh. The other, the left, is metallic, with a nonhuman wrist articulated with some kind of robotic joinery. The space between these hands sparks, suggesting

31. And where else would this sort of missive be published besides the *Chronicle of Higher Education*? See Amy Hungerford, "On Refusing to Read," *Chronicle Review,* September 11, 2016, https://www.chronicle.com /article/On-Refusing-to-Read/237717.

32. E.g., Annesha De, "Who'll Be the Winner: Human Intelligence vs. Artificial Intelligence," Fossbytes, November 10, 2015, https://fossbytes .com/co-evolution-human-intelligence-artificial-intelligence; https://www .privacytech.fr/.

33. The image comes from the illustrator Andrea Danti's portfolio on Shutterstock.

that right and left can't meet in a gesture of mutual recognition—no paradigmatic handshake of solidarity, no amorous embrace—but only as an instance of input impedance, a formative short-circuit.

It's not an easy thing to meet your maker.

In Michelangelo's version of the encounter, the human hand waits listlessly for divine jump-start, attached to body posed as if it does not yet know what it is to be turned on or off. Despite the wild power imbalance—listless flesh, on your left, omnipotence, on your right—the original version of origin par excellence is sparkless. The incremental distance implies an infinite reach of transcendent connectivity. As Robert Hertz notes in his 1909 treatise on hands: "To the right hand go honours, flattering designations, prerogatives: it acts, orders, and *takes*. The left hand, on the contrary, is despised and reduced to the role of a humble auxiliary: by itself it can do nothing; it helps, it supports, it *holds*."[34] The valuation is unfair. Both lefties and righties hold and take.

The artificial hand is another matter, indexing not connection per se but the immanence of disconnection in the very technical condition of having a hand. The hand itself is a maladroit form of original, auxiliary on/off functionality. One finger is part of an actual hand, the other is an actual switch, but the lingering issue is, which one? The spark is no longer implied, intimated in the mirroring of one hand (divine, active, creative, dexterous) with the other (auxiliary, passive, instrumental, sinister), but what must be made literal, visualized, reverse-engineered, programmed, triggered, in effect, is a kind of damaged circuitry of the human body. Or, to borrow from a recent tweet, once the things you owned, owned you; now the things you use (that you hold, that you ask for help and support), use you. What's handy—*Zuhandigkeit* (ready-to-handedness, to use Martin Heidegger's coinage)—spoils hands qua hands. It's getting harder to grasp. The left takes charge, the right points, holds the book, the telephone, ham-fisted, the match, the warm gun; the trigger finger, pressing an elevator button.

"They programmed you to think you were a human with a surgically attached computer for a hand." From a speaker in the artificial left hand attached to the protagonist, this sentence comes right after he learns he is in fact a human-looking automaton. It happens in the penultimate scene of a classic 1964 episode of *The Outer Limits*, "Demon with a Glass Hand," written by Harlan Ellison.[35] Mr. Trent is the eponymous Demon—more like Maxwell's thermodynamic particle sorter or the Socratic guidance and interruption system than one of the diabolical monsters more familiar from the series. *The Outer Limits* ran for two seasons and was scripted by some speculative fiction heavyweights. It followed an anthology structure, each episode framed by a message, a certain cybernetic conceit about the spoiling word that has particular resonance for this episode:

> There is nothing wrong with your television set. Do not attempt to adjust the picture. We are controlling transmission. If we wish to make it louder, we will bring up the volume. If we wish to make it softer, we will tune it to a whisper. We will control the horizontal. We will control the vertical. We can roll the image, make it flutter. We can change the focus to a soft blur or sharpen it to crystal clarity. For the next hour, sit quietly and we will control all that you see and hear.[36]

The program controls you, and, we repeat, there's nothing wrong with your set.

In fact, the last uncomfortable glance from Trent's would-be human love interest—Consuelo—is what's *just wrong*. The spoiling gesture, even more specifically, is marked by her hand withdrawing from his, an awkward gesture that simultaneously mirrors the co-created sympathy and repulsion on her face. Spoiler

---

35. Harlan Ellison, "Demon with a Glass Hand," *The Outer Limits,* dir. Byron Haskin, first aired October 17, 1964.

36. Ellison.

alert: stimulus aversion, automatic repulsion from functional au-
tomation, is the gesture that is most relevantly human. Consuelo
exits the uncanny valley, scampering down the steps of the same
building featured in *Blade Runner,* trailed only by biomechanical
ennui. Robot-Trent faces a spoiled millennium's worth of tedium,
waiting until the time arrives to execute his program, upload the
data payload, and reboot humanity. We at last understand what
the series narrator meant at the start when he cryptically compared the protagonist to the immortal Gilgamesh, a point reiter-
ated at the end: "Like the Eternal Man of Babylonian legend, like
Gilgamesh, one thousand plus two hundred years stretches before
Trent. Without love. Without friendship. Alone; neither man nor
machine, Waiting. Waiting for the day he will be called to free the
humans who gave him mobility. Movement, but not life."

Neither replicant nor terminator, Trent arrives from a ruined
future as an ambient program. Like Socrates's Daemon, he affects
interruptions, and, like Maxwell's, entropic sorting. "The 'Man/
machine' relationship was reversed," writes Flusser, a reorienta-
tion he already observes at effect paradigmatically in the workings
of the camera: "Man did not use machines any more but was used
by them. He became a relatively intelligent slave of relatively stupid machines."[37] ("The camera dictates a particular and specific
coordination of eye and hand, of intention and act, of theory and
practice."[38]) With tech as pervasive, animate platform—at our fingertips, as it were—humans become occasions for button-pushing,
keystrokes, and swiping gestures on assorted interfaces:

> What is immediately striking about it all is that the keys operate in a
> time unrelated to everyday human time, a time that follows another
> set of standards. For the keys move in the infinitesimal universe of
> particles, in the realm of the infinitely small, where time ignites like
> lightning. The second thing about keys is that being infinitely small

37. Flusser, *Shape of Things* (London: Reaktion, 1999), 52.
38. Flusser, "Transformance," http://muellerpohle.net/texts/project
-texts/transformance/.

by human standards, they can also cross over into the gigantic. One flick of the light switch crosses from the universe of electrons into the area in which man is the measure of all things. And one flick of another switch can explode a mountain or finish humanity off.[39]

In other words, our hero, the "last man on the earth of the future, the last hope of earth," is the command line itself, the spoiling word made artificial flesh.[40] His light-bright glass hand—sheathing variously miniscule blinking and whirring components, conspicuous for *the minute clicking of little wheels* associated with time—processes data, computes probabilities, and speaks instructions, using the classic question/answer interface. It "knows everything." Not incidentally, it makes it easy to find Trent when he removes a camouflaging glove in dark alleys and running around in the noir-style steampunk innards of the Bradbury making cat and mouse chase with the aliens from the future, the Kyben (low-budget special effects mark them with pantyhose caps and eyes smudged with ashen fluff). The hand is missing some fingers and carries a glitch—the human-machine rounding error, which spuriously partitions the human from the machine. Like a semiconductor, the flow of information moves in one direction only: "I don't know who I am, or where I've been, or where I'm going. Someone wiped my memories clean, and they tracked me down and tried to kill me. Why? Who are you? . . . And then the hand—my hand—told me what to do." Trent has a need-to-know relationship with his hand. It communicates bits of information as missing components are recovered and installed (fingers = upgrades), until the voice tells him . . . that he isn't human after all (= only an instrument), a time capsule containing all future humans compressed into data form.

Fittingly, this knowledge is hidden in his (synthetic) body—held back, as it happens, beyond our grasp—until the final (now spoiled) reveal. The Automaton from after the extinction event is

39. Flusser, *Into the Universe of Technical Images,* 23.
40. Ellison, "Demon with a Glass Hand."

wholly realized, but with functionality self-withheld. Even then, there remains but one last question: Where is everyone? Where are the billions of humans hiding from the future? Answer: the solenoid within Mr. Trent that "holds all knowledge" holds in suspension as "electrical impulses" on "a thin strand of gold-copper alloy wire." This message from the future termination point is akin to the Bottle City of Kandor in Superman comics. In effect, this data file makes Trent himself the technical parcel—the black box, the animate spoiler alert, the memeplex—that prematurely realizes what Flusser calls the universe of technical images, the "future society [that] synthesizes electronic images" as data.[41] Spoiler: rather than surrender the humans of the future to alien invaders, the leaders of the future spoiled it with a radioactive plague and "translated" themselves into the present on a zip file borne by an android. The spoiler effect is another fantastic, telematic chiasmus in which a maximalist quantity of ungraspable informationalism is translated into a series of minimal, miniaturized traumatic switches to be flicked, touched, tickled by gestures, which, as the hand says, is but "a commonplace means of preserving life" in the future. The latest in advanced data storage demands *knowing as little as possible*—to borrow from the boilerplate appended to so many spoiler alerts online. Click away now! The finger presses the button, but the inevitable extinction event is the real Master, the canceled future hidden all over the place in the present. "You may never get to touch the Master," writes Pynchon, "but you can tickle his creatures"—another paranoid message in a bottle, put to sea as well by Pynchon as by Vilém Flusser or Harlan Ellison.[42]

Programmed Algorithms replacing Literary Culture, what emerges is a phenomenology of technical images and miniaturized decisions, ubiquitous triggers—glitches, twitches, switches—minimal machines loaded with maximum potential energy, ready

---

41. Flusser, *Into the Universe of Technical Images,* 3.
42. Thomas Pynchon, *Gravity's Rainbow* (New York: Penguin, 1997), 237.

to be stupidly discharged, activated, sprung loose, when least expected. Spoiler: Chekhov's gun. What *did* you expect anyway?

The warning is, expect it everywhere—Harlan Ellison's zip-gun, for instance, which he details in his literary autobiography *Memos from Purgatory*, recounting his research among teenage hoods in New York City in the 1950s:

> The tube-rod in a coffee percolator is the barrel. Did you know it's exactly right for a .22 calibre slug? Or perhaps it's not the stem from a coffee pot. Perhaps it's a snapped-off car radio antenna. Either one will do the job. They mount it on a block of wood for a grip, with friction tape, and then they rig a rubber-band-and-metal-firing-pin device that will drive the .22 bullet down that percolator stem or antenna shell, and kill another teen-ager. What they don't bother to tell you is that a zip-gun is the most inaccurate, poorly-designed, dangerous weapon of the streets. Not only dangerous to the victim, but equally dangerous to the assailant, for too often the zip will explode in the firer's hand, too often the inaccuracy of the homemade handgun will cause an innocent bystander to be shot.[43]

Moving from zip-guns to *The Outer Limits*, miniaturized decision menaces everyone, everywhere: the glass hand, the bent twig, the elevator button, the passport photo, the lock, the wire, the doorknob, the trigger, the radioactive disease unleashed in the future, the solenoid, even the binary appearance of alien invaders, the Kyben. Their medallions anchor them in the present, Trent learns. It is "as if time were a rubber band," one explains (as Trent tortures him). They exist in the now on "an end stretched out tight." Once this link is broken, "they snap back up to the [foreclosed] future."[44] In effect, they exist precariously as an on/off switch, which, when pressed, finishes them off. Trent, too: the "human" right hand holds the gun, turns the doorknobs, presses the elevator button to speed down to the lobby to retrieve something vital from the mail slot. It yanks the chain that snuffs out the Kyben. Tellingly, the left hand—the glass hand—does not grasp at all. As a universal

43. Ellison, *Memos from Purgatory* (New York: Open Road, 2014).
44. Ellison.

computer, it encloses the sum of all knowledge with the glitch that
it carries no capacity for disclosing it. It holds nothing, yet with-
holds all. The proliferation of switches manages time until the extinction event and then flips the reboot switch on humanity. (The
time-traveling paradox would seem to demand that Mr. Trent wait
out the radioactive plague *Primer*-style in a storage locker.)

Spoiling is a platform, a programmatic glitch, and spoilers have
ontically traceable data exhaust. Here, in this narrow sense, is the
first spoiler alert, then, by internet consensus, at least:

#R:we53:-13000:uicsovax:4000009:000:301

uicsovax!hamilton Jun 8 00:47:00 1982

[SPOILER ALERT]

regarding Spock's parting gesture to McCoy, it wouldn't surprize me
if that's how they bring him back (if they do); but then, i have a low
opinion of ST's script(s). Spock's farewell to Kirk sounded pretty final to me.

wayne hamilton

decvax!pur-ee!uiucdcs!uicsovax!hamilton)[45]

Behind glass, Spock is insulated in the stupidity feedback machine, in which the supposed finality of his death in *Star Trek II:
The Wrath of Khan* (1982) from radiation poisoning instigates the
requisite suspicion from one Wayne Hamilton. However percep-
tive and perspicuous this one fan's response to the parting gesture
(uploaded data per Vulcan mind-meld into McCoy's brain-cloud),
there's no way Hamilton can know the answer one way or another,
two years before *Star Trek III: The Search for Spock* (1984) confirms the hunch. Tellingly, the fact that one viewer might correctly
intuit Spock's inevitable resurrection (I guessed it!) is ascribed to
a critical failure of writing. Yet the viewer at once flags a constitu-

45. https://groups.google.com/forum/#!msg/net.movies/c09z1
_ob—M/hTh1SpYoSa4J.

tive lack of surprise as well as a regulative, troll-like desire to ruin the experience of others (you didn't!) on borrowed moral authority from those who suffer programs and glitches.

Trigger warnings may or may not signal the same human/machine feedback problem as spoiler alerts, but wired backward. A wreck (not-) watched in reverse. (I think they do/they are, but if you think ab initio that they do not, stop reading now.) The fanlore wiki—which I report on good authority is not a reputable academic source—notes that an "early use of the term was on alt.tv.x-files. creative" in 1998: "I do not like rape stories. I do not read them. Luckily, they do not trigger me (though I'm sure they do others), but I don't like them. I would like to have been warned about this before I started."[46] Dostoevsky would not give up for anything his triggers and the seizures they auratically anticipated: "I feel entirely in harmony with myself and the whole world, and this feeling is so strong and so delightful that for a few seconds of such bliss one would gladly give up 10 years of one's life, if not one's whole life."[47] Nietzsche saw a horse being whipped in the streets of Turin and never recovered.[48] One thing is clear: preemptive signaling—alerts and warnings as aesthetic-affective boundary setting—is our new platform for experience and the wholesale wreckage of categories and criteria.

The fanlore wiki provides an excellent example of the complex logomachy hidden in this circuitry from an early trigger warning:

46. See https://fanlore.org/wiki/Trigger. There is a substantial, somewhat alarmist body of academic, quasi-academic, and journalistic materials—including readily available bibliographies—about the sociological and psychological basis of triggers, especially their role in the classroom. In this material, one quickly multiplies examples of conceptual convergence and analogies with spoilers/spoiler alerts. See, e.g., http://slideplayer.com /slide/10161940/.

47. https://www.newscientist.com/article/dn23732-mindscapes -transported-by-seizures-to-a-land-of-bliss/.

48. https://books.google.com/books?id=SAfJEptUvMUC&pg=RA1 -PT414.

I tend to argue passionately in favor of no warnings, or generalized warnings . . . and warn more specifically anyway. But I'm never sure where the line is. If I have a story that's got no "obvious" triggers (rape, incest, death, etc.) but the lead character is, say, a bigoted asshole, do I warn people that his attitudes are offensive? Or if I'm writing from the perspective of a mentally ill character, do I warn people that *that* might upset them (and yes, both of these examples are taken from stuff I've actually written in other fandoms). I mean, I know for a fact that that *would* wreck the story for many folks out there. Is it common courtesy, or is it political correctness? Where's the line?[49]

These are epiphenomenal demons of Moore's law: packets of seriality confounded by ubiquity; replay culture, streaming, and DVRs; the endless online chattersphere; USENET, the undead zone of comments sections, online fora, fandom, trolls, and bots. The sudden appearance of terrible future knowledge seems to confound present stupidities from all directions. This platform that is alarmed—altered and warned—has means and agencies. More circumspectly, they are the technical side effects of the enormous capacities of storage, information readily available at bargain-basement prices, well before our current moment.

We now return control of your television set to you. Until next week at the same time, when the control voice will take you to the Outer Limits.

49. https://fanlore.org/wiki/Trigger.

There Is Yet Insufficient Data for a Meaningful Answer: Inhumanism at the Literary Limit

AMONG ITS OTHER MERITS, Vilém Flusser's strange treatise on *vampyroteuthis infernalis* is a fable about information at the literary limit. Comparing "the vampire squid from hell" and *Homo sapiens sapiens,* he proposes a fantastic convergence that links the odd existence of a tentacled life-form, complexly equipped for probing the deep ocean, to the inhuman consequences of our emerging system of new media. Humans increasingly approximate the strategies of invertebrate life, Flusser writes:

> As our interest in objects began to wane, we created media that have enabled us to rape human brains, forcing them to store immaterial information. We have built chromatophores of our own—televisions, videos, and computer monitors that display synthetic images—with whose help broadcasters of information can mendaciously seduce their audiences.[1]

Is this assessment hyperbolic? Probably not. Recumbent with chromatophoric gadgets, humans become more and more cephalopodan, probing, probed by, and propelled through an endless ooze of immaterial information. Increasingly, our environment is, in so many words, the seemingly unfathomable abyss of Big Data plumbed fitfully by inhuman algorithms.

Like the vampyroteuthic dataverse, Big Data presents a liter-

---

1. Vilém Flusser, *Vampyroteuthis Infernalis: A Treatise, with a Report by the Institut Scientifique de Recherche Paranaturaliste* (Minneapolis: University of Minnesota Press, 2012), 67.

ary problem that defies sensible human scales.[2] Big data signals
an end game for a literary humanism that depends on the kind of
specially selected, reasonably portioned, yet easy-to-lose information anyone might come to value in the reference frame of a single
lifetime. Formerly, humans worked hard—and mostly failed—to
give their information durable form in terms of finite objects—
grasping problems, transforming "intractable things into manageable ones," coming up against the "last things" "that could not be
transformed or overcome," archiving what they found out as best
they could for later.[3] Now, things have changed; the sheer pile-
up of inexpensive, new-style stuff overwhelms us from all sides
with unmanageable nonthings "negligible from existential point
of view."[4] "Humans," returning to the ever-prescient Flusser, "no
longer realize their creative potential by struggling against the resistance of stubborn objects. . . . From now on, humans can realize
their creative potential by processing new and immaterial information" and then by selling it back at "inflated prices" to a "domi-
nated" humanity.[5] The change from handling in-formed objects to
processing an abyss of potential information is decisive. In effect,
Flusser observes a state-shift from an age when the inevitability
of further processing was not a given—when *raw data* were *not* an
oxymoron, to invoke Lisa Gitelman—to a time when it is inevitably so.[6] The idea of unprocessed information—and things which
are intractable to processing—increasingly seems like a naive ar-

2. Flusser understands the problem as one of art or artifice, but
because it concerns form, inscription, and scale, I think the literary may be
a more apt way to think about it. See also Mark McGurl, "The Posthuman
Comedy," *Critical Inquiry* 38, no. 3 (2012): 533–53.

3. Flusser, *The Shape of Things: A Philosophy of Design* (London:
Reaktion, 1999), 86.

4. Flusser, 87.

5. Flusser, *Vampyroteuthis Infernalis*, 66–67; Flusser, *Shape of Things*,
88.

6. See Lisa Gitelman, *"Raw Data" Is an Oxymoron* (Cambridge, Mass.:
MIT Press, 2013).

chaism to those saturated with so much potential information.[7] Now, every nonthing comes preformed with massive quantities of metadata—date and time stamps, above all else—a vapor trail of data-as-waste, which our insidious gadgets leave us willy-nilly, whether it matters or not. Mostly not—we hope.

Hovering in the background here is the "friendly reminder" from new media studies that data are always already "cooked" and never entirely "raw," an allusion to Claude Levi-Strauss's structuralist classic *The Raw and the Cooked,* invoked to emphasize that data are cultural, not natural, phenomena.[8] One way or another, data always come prepared, it's held. Yet, following Levi-Strauss, raw and cooked are *linked* empirical categories, and cooking is the middle phase—"a form of mediation," he repeatedly intones.[9] Perhaps it's worth pressing a poststructuralist point: *raw* is a discourse effect of *cooked*; the unmarked/marked pair is mutually constitutive. *Raw* is more than relational, in other words; it's also meditational and semiconductive. In later work, Levi-Strauss nuances his culinary–cultural matrix, adding gradients extending from *almost raw* to *more than cooked* and including such additional states as *burnt* and *rotten* as well as *bland* and *spicy*.[10] The in-

7. Rather than nature/culture, the problem of big data concerns singular/plural. Tellingly, *data* is seldom encountered in singular form. There's so much of it. To revisit a critical commonplace, the singular *datum* means *given* in Latin in the sense of an input available for (further) processing. An Input-Output-Input model: *freely it has been given to you, freely give.* Date has a similar root, as Daniel Rosenberg reminds us, and *metadata* comes semantically overburdened. See Daniel Rosenberg, "Data before the Fact," in Gitelman,*"Raw Data" Is an Oxymoron,* 15–40.

8. Claude Lévi-Strauss, *The Raw and the Cooked* (London: Pimlico, 1994). See Gitelman,*"Raw Data" Is an Oxymoron,* 2: "Raw data is both an oxymoron and a bad idea. On the contrary, data should be cooked with care"—the TED-like assertion by Geoffrey C. Bowker serves Gitelman's collection more as a motto than a thesis. See esp. his afterword, 167–72.

9. Claude Levi-Strauss, *The Raw and the Cooked* (Chicago: University of Chicago Press, 1983), 1, 64.

10. See, e.g., Claude Levi-Strauss, *From Honey to Ashes* (New York: HarperCollins, 1973).

evitability of such category shifting—changes in state from *given* to *taken,* for example—indicates that, despite appearances, categorical terms like *data* have little self-sufficiency. If *data* implies something like *available for further processing,* it manifests the same problems as *guest* and *host,* eating off one another. In the beginning, as Michel Serres reminds us, comes the parasite: "Real production is unexpected and improbable, it overflows with information and is always immediately parasited."[11] The break in the flow—the interruption—is formative static.

In other words, data don't need to be raw to be considered oxymoronic. Contradiction is already on board, yoking the sharp and the dull, as the etymology of *oxymoron* suggests. Raw data are a kind of pleonastic oxymoron, presupposing multiplicity as accumulation—processing plural to singular into a set, a matrix, a database, and so forth. The ambition is to fit all data—to process everything; *they* becomes *it.* Switching to singular, then, data come always already sharpened, the argument goes; data are less raw than constitutively messy. Raw and/or cooked, the massive amounts of static implicated in inhuman scales make archival issues conspicuous in several ways. For better or worse, hangovers of obsolete form—skeuomorphs—hover about our metaphors about managing data, information, and knowledge. Google isn't an archive per se. It's a inhuman finding aid for making sense of its monstrously expanding archives. For all their ubiquity, analogies drawn between in-formed objects with finite capacities and the nebulous communication dataverse designated by the cloud are also simultaneously monstrous and clumsy.[12] Humans once fashioned in-formed objects with archival powers, Flusser points

11. Michel Serres, *The Parasite* (Minneapolis: University of Minnesota Press, 2007), 4.

12. See Dean Lockwood and Rob Coley, *Cloud Time* (London: Zero, 2012). Instead of reserving for raw something the illusion of uninterrupted, authentic experience, the agency of "fossil data" resembles the heap and its noises—the clamor of being.

out in his fable, for orientation and memory—the bent twig used to indicate a direction on a path, for instance. Once upon a time, we gathered info to disseminate it and fabricated artificial memories. Now that ever larger quantities overwhelm our objectworld, we require special, systematic finding aids—search engines, above all. Input comes prior to information. Consider the rise of the algorithm along these lines: algorithms require archives to function, and we trade on a host of archival metaphors to talk about them, yet they are not archives. Instead, they are methods for producing systematic outputs—for cooking data, so to speak—recipes that get themselves archived and that need various archives to work. It may be that "new-style information," as Flusser puts it, is "negligible from the existential point of view," yet does this existential melancholy even matter if every ephemeral state is now collectible and available for potential use?[13]

Tracking a genealogy for making literary sense of spoilers and scales of input and output takes us back to the future, back to modernist concerns with deep time, impossible author functions, and maximal and minimal audience structures. The spoiler archive is a futurist ersatz-archive, search engines engineered for grasping what's "impossible to get a hold of," processed at inhuman scales and expanding reference beyond the Anthropocene. The murky abyss, as it were, includes speculation about deep futurity, time after human extinction, for instance, that draws on the scientific extrapolations of cosmology. It also confronts the technically assisted observation of a "reality anterior to the emergence of the human species—or even anterior to every recognized form of life on earth," as Quentin Meillassoux characterizes it. The arche-fossil that Meillassoux describes—clearly rooted in modern knowledge of inhuman timescales advanced by geology and platetectonics—is also a fossil of the future, "designat[ing] the material support on the basis of which the experiments that yield estimates of ances-

13. Flusser, *Shape of Things*, 86.

tral phenomena proceed—for example, an isotope whose rate of radioactive decay we know, or the luminous emission of a star that informs us as to the date of its formation."[14] Such ersatz-archives are not merely eccentric; they exit the orbit of the human-scale archiving practices altogether. Seeing and hearing by technical means—devising techniques of observation, experiment, and reflection—is the crux of what Siegfried Zielinski sees as Flusser's media philosophy and also the lodestone of his own project of media variantology: "technical media had been a pile, a treasure of possibilities (or perhaps better: potentialities), which permanently had to be explored, every day and everyday new."[15] This chapter takes such variantology as occasion for literary speculation about the scalar implications of a long inhuman turn in modernity, administering complexity of temporality as an inevitable encounter with entropy and expiration—navigating the abyss of expired databases, dated theories, and dead links.

"Take your books of mere poetry and prose; let me read a timetable, with tears of pride."[16]

So says the hero of G. K. Chesterton's *The Man Who Was Thursday* observing not only that time is information but also that it has affective texture. Let me name one of the commonplaces of the literary modern: searching for aesthetic possibilities in a newly regimented world. As modern time becomes increasingly administered on and by the clock, human timescales—seconds, minutes, years—become increasingly remote, displaced from fundamental science first by deep geological time and then by the discoveries of quantum mechanics and scientific cosmology. The new inter-

14. Quentin Meillassoux, *After Finitude* (London: Continuum, 2008).

15. "Vilém Flusser: A Brief Introduction to His Media Philosophy," https://monoskop.org/images/4/4b/Flussers_View_on_Art_MECAD _Online_Seminar.pdf. See also Siegfried Zielinski, *Deep Time of the Media: Toward an Archaeology of Hearing and Seeing by Technical Means* (Cambridge, Mass.: MIT Press, 2008).

16. G. K. Chesterton, *The Man Who Was Thursday* (New York: Penguin, 2011), 40.

vals of physics are so short that they are impossible to relate to, whereas the tempos of cosmos are so long that they prove similarly inhuman.

The literary modern affords special epistemological status to unforeseen circumstances beyond human control. This chapter concerns the collection of literary knowledge in inhuman quantities and the literary implications of scalar shifts in information—including temporal information—in modernity. In particular, it explores modernist interest in "collecting" absurdly long time frames, scales of the deep future that dwarf another standard developed by remapping the psychologized, subjectivized mind with the topographies of the classical epic (i.e., on Bloom's day, June 16, 1904, or Quentin's day, June 2, 1910, or Mrs. Dalloway's day). In this regard, H. G. Wells's 802,701 A.D. is a critical search result for an alternative inhuman (in-Bloomian, sub-Quentinian, ex-Dallowegian) modernism that has ongoing implications. In *The Time Machine,* for instance, his thought experiments in extreme futurism reveal a decidedly literary pedigree for the engineered machines currently plying the World Wide Web.[17] Considering the Wellsian search engines alongside other cognate versions proposed by Isaac Asimov, J. G. Ballard, and others, I argue that a conceivable end of human knowledge frameworks—the "death of the sun," using the critical shorthand proposed by Jean-François Lyotard—provides something like a new modern sublime: the cold return of the inert and the quiet, the background temperature of outer space, the unlit, unvoiced stone, the exhaustion of exhaustion. Here we might find the inhuman happiness that follows postmodern nihilism and the recent consolations of the archive: never give up on a better past.

H. G. Wells is the ideal literary instrument for thinking about human and inhuman time for two reasons, first, his literary name prepossessed by the idea of generation. You see this in his own

17. H. G. Wells, *The Time Machine* (New York: W. W. Norton, 2008).

writings when Wells discusses his relation to other writers, in particular, in his *Experiment in Autobiography* composing the Wellsian brain.[18] What Wells does again and again is to place his powers of attention out of the frame of the contemporary. Despite the popular reputation of Wells as a visionary, the purported originator of modern science fiction appears to suffer, however ironically, from the maxim that nothing ages faster than the future. That so many of his visions of the future "came true"—as is often remarked— seems of little moment in this regard. To the midcentury professoriate, Wells *feels* older than Henry James, the author who's a full generation younger; Wellsian style seems more *dated*. More of our times; less our contemporary. What can datedness mean, as Justin Clemens and Dominic Pettman have well observed, when we're caught in "the great aesthetic whirlpool [that] neither validates nor rejects any particular epoch"?[19] This sense of Wellsian datedness may follow from his status as a name on the edge of this whirlpool. His search engines are calibrated to overleap generational scales; his alternative histories report to impossible future readerships. One might say that Wells was interested in the formula generation after generation not so much as a commonplace of sequence but as an inhuman problem: what happens to the idea of generation after generation is a zombie concept.

I'm thinking especially of *The Sleeper Awakes,* in which the protagonist goes into a trance in 1897, sleeps through the Martian wars, and wakes up centuries later to find that through compounded interest, he literally owns the future.[20] I'm thinking of the sleeper, the time traveler, the subject of *The World Set Free,* the Wellsian premise of "humanity surviving extinction, of overvaulting the end of time and historical epochs, not toward the future or

18. H. G. Wells, *Experiment in Autobiography* (Boston: Little, Brown, 1962).

19. Justin Clemens and Dominic Pettman, *Avoiding the Subject: Media, Culture, and the Object* (Amsterdam: University of Amsterdam, 2004), 33.

20. H. G. Wells, *The Sleeper Awakes* (New York: Penguin, 2005).

the past, but toward the heart itself of time and history," to borrow some Agambenian language.[21] Before spooling to the end, some preliminary remarks about modernism and time—historicity, contemporaneity, futurity, and the concept of generation itself—may be in order. In *Graphs, Maps and Trees*, Franco Moretti notices three intervals of literary time, which he imports from the Annales school.[22] At one end of the spectrum is the very short term—the bread and butter of modernist studies: the event, the break, or the rupture, the instantaneous experience of novelty, the aesthetic effect just there that changes everything. At the other side is the very long term, the epoch, the era, or the longue durée: the period-spanning historical thesis that in its own way is another second mainstay of modernist scholarship.

Or else, maybe more accurately, one could say that the very short is constitutive of modernist studies, whereas the very long is regulative of it. With all the emphasis on temporal particularities and generalities, we modernist scholars have ill-served the middle term, the temporal span that Moretti calls the cycle. Cycles, as he has it, "constitute temporary structures within the historical flow." These represent an "unstable" "border country" between the incremental and structureless shock of the new designated by the event and the static and overly structured critical forensics designated by the epoch.[23] It's no secret that what Moretti means by the cycle, his so-called temporary structure, is more commonly understood as genre. In so many words, genres are "morphological arrangements that last in time," durable but never permanent literary dispositions for, say, imperial gothic or teenage vampire abstinence novels.[24] In his examples derived from nineteenth-century cases, they last between twenty-five and thirty years. Whether

21. Giorgio Agamben, *Idea of Prose* (Albany: SUNY University Press, 1995), 88.

22. Franco Moretti, *Graphs, Maps, and Trees* (London: Verso, 2005), 14.

23. Moretti.

24. Moretti, 17.

or not the life cycle of genres accelerates with the technomedial evolutions of the twentieth century is a key question for Moretti's methodology. Isn't the Morettian cycle in fact the Agambenian whirlpool? I want to put pressure on Moretti's insight by making an observation: thinking about genre as the life cycle of forms—beginnings and endings, birth and death—inevitably calls forth something like generation. Genres, generations. The beginnings and endings of genres resemble the birth and death of generations by more than mere homology. A generation signals a cohort born at roughly the same time, shaped by the same generic conditions, events, shared forms of technomediality: "each generation tallies its new talent and catalogues its new forms and epochal tendencies in art and thought."[25] It is no coincidence, I submit, that the conventional measure afforded to a generation—twenty-five to thirty years—is basically the span of time that Moretti apportions to the life of a genre.[26]

And yet, the ultimate distant reader, the computational knowledge engine, Multivac, in the end, at the end of Isaac Asimov's "The Last Question," can at last report the hard-won findings to . . . no generation, the universe being finally over.[27] Jean-François Lyotard writes that, with the inevitable exhaustion of the sun—4.57 billion years and counting—comes the death of death.[28] And, is that not a good thing? A happy end, in a manner of thinking, to thinking? *Fiat lux* and nowhere to report the search results. Here we find the nonhuman "happiness" that follows postmodern nihilism, a happy refusal of the consolations of the archive. Don't go back to the airport flyover, it tells us, like the prisoner in Chris

25. Agamben, *Idea of Prose*, 87.
26. The classic study of this concept is Karl Mannheim, "The Problem of Generations," in *Essays on the Sociology of Knowledge by Karl Mannheim*, ed. P. Kecskemeti, 276–320 (New York: Routledge and Kegan Paul, 1952).
27. Isaac Asimov, "The Last Question," in *The Complete Stories*, vol. 1, 290–300 (New York: Broadway, 1990).
28. Jean-François Lyotard, *The Inhuman: Reflections on Time* (Stanford, Calif.: Stanford University Press, 1992), 8–9.

Marker's *La Jeté* (1962), blocked for the future because he can't give up on his desire for a better past.

That said, our blueprints for the administration of inhuman time include J. G. Ballard and Isaac Asimov: Ballard to understand the consequences of an inevitably minimal unhuman end to human knowledge frameworks, Asimov to formulate a critical concept of the literary as a thought experiment about maximal knowledge. I file this report, however truncated and schematic, to pursue a contrarian path for criticism through a vast science fiction/speculative fiction corpus, a path avoiding the familiar Heinlein–Dick "postmodernist" axis. Instead, Asimov and Ballard get pride of place in a paleofuturist genealogy of speculative, intellectual modernist outliers writing impossible scenarios about unhuman literary machinery, a genealogy that stretches from Ursula K. Le Guin to Olaf Stapledon to H. G. Wells, among whom we could certainly count Jorge Luis Borges and Franz Kafka. The prolific Asimov has his pulp, genre-fiction bona-fides and hard SF credentials, but his emigrant background (a child of Yiddish speakers, a man without papers from an impossible cultural-linguistic zone) and his standing as a committed scientific popularizer and as an actual professor of the natural sciences pushes his profile beyond the frothy space operas, interplanetary romances, and rocket and ray-gun escapades of many of his cold war contemporaries.

But, before we crank up the dials of Asimovian maximalism, first Ballardian minimalism. Ballard's career stretches from the mid-1950s to the day before the present. And he may be even more difficult to classify. Less interested in the gear of hard science fiction and its attendant idiom of techno-Benthamism, Ballard liked to claim kinship with the surrealists: "My science fiction was not about outer space," he wrote, "but about psychological change, psychological space."[29] Sometimes a bright line is drawn between Ballard's early, more "conventional" SF stuff and his later, more ex-

29. J. G. Ballard, *Millennium People* (New York: W. W. Norton, 2011), 4.

perimental, and thus more "literary," work. Nonetheless, Ballard
manages across the range of his oeuvre to remain obsessively interested in the near-term catastrophic end: the collapsing inner
space of human knowledge systems. His first four novels all de-
scribe the psychological consequences of various transformations
of the Earth into a hostile, alien environment; his later fiction
seems to come to a conclusion that this conceit was a superflu-
ous fantasy. The Earth was already transformed: "Earth is the only
alien planet," he claimed, famously, "and the future is five minutes
away." "Our concepts of past, present and future are bring forced
to revise themselves," he writes. "The past, in social and psychological terms, became a casualty of Hiroshima and the nuclear
age. . . . The future is ceasing to exist, devoured by the voracious
present."[30]

He's the past master of what we could call stalking inner space,
a term he's credited with inventing in 1962: the mind scanning the
tuner for weaker and weaker information signals.[31] Despite the
inherent minimalism of the activity, it yields surprisingly warped
and uncanny encounters as in Tarkovsky's *Stalker* (1979). "We
have annexed the future into the present," Ballard writes: "Options
multiply around us, and we live in an almost infantile world where
any demand, any possibility, whether for life-styles, travel, sexual
roles and identities, can be satisfied instantly."[32] Ballard's fiction is
full of search engines stalking five minutes into the future. The instrument panel choked with dust and filth, social and psychological channels clogged with chatter, Ballard's fiction still probes for
messages. One such story set "five minutes in the future" is "The
Message from Mars" (1992). The tale has an interplanetary space
crew of celebrity astronauts returning from Mars in a hermetically

30. J. G. Ballard, introduction to *Crash* (New York: Picador 2001), 4.
31. See Samuel Francis, *The Psychological Fictions of J. G. Ballard* (London: Bloombury, 2011), 65–66.
32. Ballard, introduction to *Crash*.

sealed, self-sustaining ship.[33] Parked on the landing strip after the seemingly triumphant voyage, the passengers refuse to disembark, protected from the entreaties from without by an impenetrable space-age ceramic shell, sustained by a reactor and a well-stocked larder. "Rejecting the [outer] world with a brief wave," they choose instead to live out their lives in "a sealed [inner] world, immune to any presses from within and without," for reasons impossible to clarify by observers outside.[34] A capsule full of Bartlebys or Garbos. An allegory of the current media ecology rests on the passengers' petulant refusal to play along with a massive propaganda-and-PR apparatus setup to record and hype their mission for a global audience, a noisy Space Family Robinson reality show trading on all-too-facile plotlines and debased audience expectations.

Inner space is quieter than outer space. The allegorical capacity become unglued with the passage of time. Elsewhere, Ballard notes the futility of escape from the autonomous life pod:

> In the past we have always assumed that the external world around us represented reality, however confusing or uncertain, and that the inner world of our minds, its dreams, hopes, ambitions, represented the realm of fantasy and the imagination. These roles, it seems to me, have been reversed. The most prudent and effective of dealing with the world around us is to assume that it is a complete fiction—conversely, the one small node of reality left to us is inside our own heads.[35]

In the end, after NASA itself passes into history, the ship—decommissioned, forgotten, its life support still operational—ends up an inscrutable piece of hulking junk deposited on a parking lot. Another mobile home in a trailer park. A graduate student eventually rediscovers the ship there and hooks up various instruments and magnetic imaging equipment—search engines of a certain kind:

33. Ballard, "The Message from Mars," in *The Complete Stories of J. G. Ballard,* 1175–83 (New York: W. W. Norton, 2009).

34. Ballard, 1178.

35. Ballard, introduction to *Crash,* 5.

> An aged couple, Commander John Merritt and Dr Vanentina Tsarev, now in their late eighties, sat in their small cabins, hands folded on their laps. There were no books or ornaments beside their simple beds. Despite their extreme age they were clearly alert, tidy and reasonably well nourished. Most mysteriously, across their eyes moved the continuous play of a keen and amused intelligence.[36]

Despite the sensitivity of the instruments, able to pick up the smallest details of their eye movements, I find the meaning of this scene inscrutable. It has something of the quality of Ti and Bo and the Heaven's Gate Cult. Or Pong. I don't question the veracity of the data about their "keen and amused intelligence," only that the meaning of the observation remains a cipher. It could be fruitfully matched with another mysterious comment Ballard made about the task of the writer:

> What is the main task facing the writer? . . . The writer knows nothing any longer. He has no moral stance. He offers the reader the contents of his own head, a set of options and imaginative alternatives. His role is that of the scientist, where on safari or in his laboratory, faced with an unknown terrain or subject.[37]

Here we can turn from the minimalist response conveyed by Ballard's minimalist time machine to a short detour Asimovian search engines working maximal overdrive. First, a short detour back to Wells, who was, not surprisingly, a professed influence of both writers.

In *The Time Machine,* the Time Traveler jumps ahead to 802,701 A.D. The number is big, but in a specific, almost too ordinary and uneventful way—a bigger version of the famous 42 in *Hitchhiker's Guide to the Galaxy,* to which I'll come back shortly. It is as if evolutionary, epochal time, scaled for charting the origin of species, has been tacked on to the historical measure of a human lifetime, as in the joke about a museum guard at the natural history museum who tells visitors that the brontosaurus bones are 150 mil-

---

36. Ballard, "Message from Mars," 1182–83.
37. Ballard, introduction to *Crash,* 5–6.

lion and five years old . . . because he's been working there for five years. The number signals, as it were, enough lapsed time for class difference, that is, the historical driver, to take on irreparably evolutionary form. Nearly a million years hence, with no other legacy of humanity to speak of, the over- and underclass of economic modernity have branched into separate species, the Morlocks and the Eloi. The ironic twist is, of course, that the descendants of the upper classes have become the food source for the proles.

While the main interest of the novel may rest in this inversion, I'm more interested in an odd scene at the end of the novel. With allegory seemingly laid to one side, the search engine pushes forward to the end of the spool, 30 million years ahead. Here, on a desolate beach, the Time Traveler observes the final sunset:

> Suddenly [he reports] I noticed that the circular westward outline of the sun had changed. . . . The darkness grew apace; a cold wind began to blow in freshening gusts from the east. . . . From the edge of the sea came a ripple and whisper. Beyond these lifeless sounds the world was silent. . . . All the sounds of man, the bleating of sheep, the cries of birds, the hum of insects, the stir that makes the background of our lives—all that was over. . . . I saw the black central shadow of the eclipse sweeping towards me. In another moment the pale stars alone were visible. All else was rayless obscurity. The sky was absolutely black.[38]

This could be described as an early scene of secular, planetary snuff. Particular details to notice are the dynamic of information and noise. The time machine is, above all, an observational machine, a search engine, tasked with uncovering improbable results. The final fade-out is interesting only for its minimalism: it reports all that isn't heard, the lack of murmurs and mumbles; bleating, bird sounds, and buzzing. Curiously, even muted nonnoise counts as noise in this context. The only information is visual, minimal light inscribing the landscape as if on a photographic plate, the human observer machine, a camera basically, placed before a de-

38. Wells, *The Time Traveler* (New York: Penguin, 2005), 98.

cidedly unhuman end, affording the time of one last, noneschato-
logical long exposure. In any sense, save for a presence that stands
in for the author function, there is nothing to be known and no audience structure to know it. This unvoiced stone under a burned-
out ember says even less than Ozymandias. Without belaboring
the paradoxes of observation, Wells's point is that the meaningful
human condition ended uneventfully some time before during the
span of eight hundred thousand odd years between the present
and the Morlock–Eloi scene. This final sunset is a quarrel with the
humanness of endings as such.

Asimov also takes an even longer view. Most famously, his
Foundation series—in fact, a cluster of interlinked stories and
novels—follows through on a logic of temporal maximalism,
stretching over thousands of years into the future. Fans have
pegged 25,621 A.D. as the latest date referenced in the series, but
it is a bit confusing, because new calendars are introduced at several junctures in the series.[39] Furthermore, the entire sequence
is menaced by the threat of information death, the edifice of human knowledge slouching into ruinous quagmires of ignorance,
coming epochs when even the measurement of history becomes
impossible. Asimov uses robots, institutions, corporations, and
other durable nonhuman dispositions to overcome the narrative
limitations of the human life-span. I'll spare the intricacies of a
work conceived as an intergalactic retelling of Edward Gibbons's
Decline and Fall of the Roman Empire. I only want to touch on two
elements of Foundation. Each in its own way takes the form of
mystified literary scholarship: the theoretical-concept of psychohistory and the project of a reference work called Encyclopedia
Galactica. In The Time Machine, the traveler goes forward to discover increasing discontinuity between what he observes and human beings and their knowledge frameworks. The scene in the

39. See Attila Torkos, Timeline for Robots and Foundation Universe,
https://www.sikander.org/foundation.php.

disused museum is paradigmatic in both Wells and the dystopian tradition. In Asimov, who is more sanguine about humanity's prospects than either Wells or Ballard, psychohistory and the *Encyclopedia Galactica* are conceived of as two durable forms extending the continuity of human knowledge frames beyond the natural life-span. Psychohistory is essentially an extrapolative form of social science—the wisdom of crowds writ large. A computational concept engine gathers massive amounts of data about human behavior; it uses its databases to calculate future human history. The more massive the data set, the more predictive it gets. Eventually, psychohistorians determine that humanity is doomed to enter a catastrophic phase, a ten-thousand-year span of stupidity, and conceive of an enterprise to preserve knowledge and mitigate against the hazards of this epoch. They set out to compile a massively comprehensive *Encyclopedia Galactica* to preserve all knowledge. This task, it is said, has the power to shorten the projected dark age by a factor of 10. The efforts of the galactic encyclopedists consume the resources of an entire planet where they are eventually exiled. In effect, the planet itself is co-opted into a giant knowledge engine, planetary size.

Let's explore the literary dimensions of these two fictional superliterary projects and some "real-world" cognates of them. Since Asimov, the *Encyclopedia Galactica* fantasy—humanity preserved through a redemptive ark of comprehensive and curated knowledge—is a pervasive meme. It plays no small part in inspiring the Wikipedia phenomenon, for instance. Douglas Adams's *Hitchhiker's Guide to the Galaxy* was a fairly self-conscious parody of it, too, a kind of *Encyclopedia Galactica for Dummies*. Allegedly filched from galactic encyclopedists, the *Guide,* Adams writes, "has many omissions and contains much that is apocryphal, or at least wildly inaccurate." Of course, one doesn't need a science fiction frame to recognize that the encyclopedia from Diderot forward is in itself motivated by a principle of epistemological maximalism as an almost manic drive. In terms of Wikipedia, I think it is safe to say that Asimov would be aghast at its open-source editing imperatives and the knee-jerk distrust of primary expert knowledge enshrined in its practices. Asimov was open source when it came to mass data collection but left the analysis, the computational psychohistory, to the positronic brain.

Asimov's related Multivac stories, a different fictional world from the Foundation series, show the fault lines of the project. In effect, Multivac draws together the two strands of inhuman humanism and puts them in a black box: first, massive information collection of the past, and second, oracle-like analysis and computational prediction of the future. As a fictional computer, the physiognomy of Multivac differs from both familiar archetypes: the humanoid robot, automaton-doppelgänger with a body and the glorified space nanny, identified with the space ship itself, charged with holding steady on the steering wheel, managing human life support for interstellar express. As a knowledge engine, Multivac is a cipher for the author function itself, I submit, a disembodied search engine for information. Like Wells's Time Machine, Asimov's very long timescales and machines to probe them can be read as thought experiments about extreme configurations of author functions and impossible audience structures.

Ending 10 million times farther in the future than *The Time Machine,* the Multivac story called "The Last Question" (1956) surely has the record for one of longest time frames ever conceived in fiction (and as such the least Aristotelian ever written).[40] It concerns a succession of Multivac responses to the question about the ultimate fate of the universe. Asimov gives the question both a cybernetic spin (What happens at the end of information?) and a thermodynamic one (Can entropy be reversed?). In seven vignettes spaced over vast segments of cosmological time from May 21, 2061, to the event of would-be entropy death, 10 trillion year later, seven varieties of this question are put to the machine and its successors.

40. Isaac Asimov, "The Last Question," *Science Fiction Quarterly,* November 1956.

Six times, the only answer returned is "THERE IS AS YET INSUF-
FICIENT DATA FOR A MEANINGFUL ANSWER." The final time the
question is asked, human beings and their evolutionary progeny are
long gone, no data are left to be collected, and all is "completely correlated and put together in all possible relationships." The seventh
computational engine—existing only in hyperspace, an information-
processing entity akin to "a computer . . . far less than was a man to
Man"—achieves total knowledge against the backdrop of entropy
death. Asimov writes, "There was now no man to whom AC might
give the answer of the last question. No matter. The answer—by
demonstration—would take care of that, too." Given the ingredients
of (1) omniscience and (2) the universe's absolute nullity, that answer is—you probably guessed it—let there be light. A clever trick.
The clue in the setup is the idea that the answer would come by
demonstration, with no information left, and no matter, this is the
only possible thing to say and to do. There is only one question to
ask at the end of the universe: what's next?

If *Hitchhiker's Guide to the Galaxy* anticipates Wikipedia, con-
sciously or unconsciously, Asimov's futurist engineered artifacts
and computational knowledge machines gesture toward the internet. They point to one of the constitutive problems concerning
the kind of epistemological maximalism that the internet signifies,
namely, interface, instrumentation, and computation—in a word,
intelligence. How do you put the question and calibrate it to get
back a meaningful answer from the accumulation of vast amounts
of mostly undigested chatter, that is, the stuff people have seen
fit to upload? You've heard the one about a million monkeys with
a million typewriters eventually writing the complete works of
Shakespeare. The internet, so goes a well-known joke, proves this
to be false. One can think of the internet as a vast assemblage of
information debris: like the dumpster behind your apartment clot-
ted with garbage, phonebooks, office materials, and the occasional
appointment calendar and obsolescent Filofax. It started as a flo-
tilla of documents lashed together by hyperlinks—various digital
flotsam, jetsam, ligan, deposited, jettisoned, discarded, claimed,

derelicted, who can say. In the early going—its incunabulum era perhaps—this assemblage of documents was countable and thus indexable. In 1993, the number of websites was in the hundreds; one year later, they numbered in the tens of thousands; today, Google estimates that the web contains 1 trillion links.[41]

The first search engines were simply efforts to measure the size of the information content of the web by tracing out all the links. For a while, the size was manageable, monitored by individuals who could be likened to Alexander and Bertram, the faithful attendants of the earliest Multivac. Their nonliterary cognates authored their own indexes, portals, and directories—"Jerry and David's Guide to the World Wide Web," the ancestor of Yahoo!, is one such example.[42] This phase ended quickly. After the internet became too big to be overseen by anyone began the phase of automated web bots, which traced out the links and the search engines that allowed human users to search for key words in this mess, the same way a search feature works on their word processing program. Even here, the results were quickly too numerous. At last, Google's algorithm came. Like its predecessors, it trawled for links—continuously scanning the cached snapshot of the internet stored on its servers. Then, and this is the key part, it ranked the results, using algorithms designed to assign each page with a ranked value based on the "quality" of its links. The most linked links ruled. In high school, the popular kids aren't the ones with the most friends but the ones with the most popular friends. Google is the same. In other words, it may not be the Multivac, precisely, but Google applies its own psychohistorical principle of massification, namely, popularity. The most likely answer is the one the most people like. Google is a hide-and-seek machine: very

41. http://googleblog.blogspot.com/2008/07/we-knew-web-was-big.html.

42. Andrew Clark, "How Jerry's Guide to the World Wide Web Became Yahoo," *Guardian,* February 1, http://www.guardian.co.uk/business/2008/feb/01/microsoft.technology.

good at finding what's well found already and very bad at finding what's very well hidden. All this tremendous expansion signals surface area and no depth. The deep web is a myth.

Now, in the contest for the title of real-life Multivac, there's a new arrival, something called WolframAlpha. It is already been described as an un-Google. What is it? If you type in its text box, What are you? WolframAlpha replies, I am a computational knowledge engine.[43] If you follow up with, What is computational knowledge? it answers, not altogether helpfully, That which I endeavor to compute. This circularity is instructive in its way, for computable knowledge is, in a sense, as computable knowledge does. WolframAlpha aims to treat information as information; as such, it's only interested in material that can be subjected to processing, calculation, or analysis rather than simply Google's hide-and-seek game of searching the static of the internet universe for signals. Thus it is necessary for WolframAlpha to maintain an internal storehouse of refereed expert-level knowledge ready made for computational machinery to process it. In other words, like Asimov's Encyclopedists, it pursues a curatorial agenda led by experts on its own planet. Here's how the WolframAlpha site explains the mission:

> We aim to collect and curate all objective data; implement every known model, method, and algorithm; and make it possible to compute whatever can be computed about anything. Our goal is to build on the achievements of science and other systematizations of knowledge to provide a single source that can be relied on by everyone for definitive answers to factual queries.[44]

One interesting side of the maximalist project is the decision to make its interface communicate through "free form natural language input." The theory for this seems to have as much to do with

---

43. http://www.wolframalpha.com/input/?i=what+are+you.
44. In 2009, this was the answer. As of 2019, it's this: "Fundamentally, it is the vast collection of quantities and facts that I provide, compare, and calculate for my users." http://www.wolframalpha.com/input/?i=What+is +computational+knowledge.

the interface between experts and nonexperts as it follows from the sense that the meta-language between the various disciplines of knowledge can be none other than natural language. "For academic purposes, WolframAlpha is a primary source"; consequently, unlike Google, but like the Asimovian computers of pop culture, it is personified.[45]

WolframAlpha is a "citable author," so notes the FAQ, as a quasi-legal tidbit for educators and researchers.[46] If you ask this literary construct, the same question asked the Multivac, How can the net amount of entropy of the universe be massively decreased? It answers the same way: THERE IS AS YET INSUFFICIENT DATA FOR A MEANINGFUL ANSWER.[47] If you ask it, What is the Answer to the Ultimate Question of Life, the Universe, and Everything? it answers, 42.[48] I take these answers to mean not that WolframAlpha thinks like Multivac—or Deep Thought—but that its programmers are aware of their literary or pop cultural pedigree. The WolframAlpha FAQ comments that "when computers were first imagined, it was almost taken for granted that they would eventually have the kinds of question-answering capabilities that we now begin to see in WolframAlpha."[49] "Is WolframAlpha an artificial intelligence?" then—a term I don't find helpful in this discussion and have so far avoided, but one WolframAlpha's website summons:

> It's much more an engineered artifact than a humanlike artificial intelligence. Some of what it does—especially in language understanding—may be similar to what humans do. But its primary objective is to do directed computations, not to act as a general intelligence.[50]

45. http://www.wolframalpha.com/about.html.
46. http://www.wolframalpha.com/about.html.
47. http://www.wolframalpha.com/input/?i=How+can+the+net +amount+of+entropy+of+the+universe+be+massively+decreased%3F.
48. http://www.wolframalpha.com/input/?i=What+is+the+Answer +to+the+Ultimate+Question+of+Life%2C+the+Universe%2C+and +Everything%3F+.
49. http://www.wolframalpha.com/about.html.
50. http://www.wolframalpha.com/about.html.

It makes sense to me to think of WolframAlpha as the conditions the author function finds itself in when facing trillions of elements of data: the black-boxed front end is less artificial intelligence than it is engineered artifact for detecting semiotic red shift.

Bruno Latour's conception of "black boxing" usefully names the discursive imperative operating here, through which, in Latour's words, "scientific and technical work is made invisible by its own success. When a machine runs efficiently, when a matter of fact is settled, one need focus only on its inputs and outputs and not on its internal complexity. Thus paradoxically, the more science and technology succeed, the more opaque and obscure they become."[51] In a sense, "black boxing" explains the end user's phenomenological situation in which technologies are routinized and made normative "no matter how controversial their history, how complex their inner-workings, how large the commercial or academic networks that hold them in place."[52] Open this black box and peak under the hood and, as I have been suggesting, you'll find the component dreamwork organized around a mass-mediated postliterary fantasy. Furthermore, the engineered artifact massively mystifies the audience structures comprising it. Audience structures are not—or they are not simply—recording machines, all storage capacity and no processing power. Rather, they might be conceived of as explicit and implicit representations of mass-mediated reception, intake rendered by means of various spatial and temporal metaphorics. The internet itself is, along these lines, a specialized audience structure. On the internet, everyone is an author, and therefore no one is an Author: the scriveners rule with squatters' rights and Bartleby-like truculence. Down with the jargon of first modernist technoauthenticity in time and space; think only of the psychohistorical predicament of readers and authors facing textual overload.

51. Bruno Latour, *Pandora's Hope* (Cambridge, Mass.: Harvard University Press, 1999), 304.

52. Bruno Latour, *Science in Action* (Cambridge, Mass.: Harvard University Press, 1988), 3.

The thread that connects Asimov and Ballard here is their fascination with audience structures, maximal and minimal. Asimov's "The Last Question" identifies a point of singularity between maximum authorial capacity—the supraliterary computational Author-God who knows and has read everything—and the minimal audience structure that there are no readers left. Once the *Encyclopedia Galactica* is completed, the world necessarily ends . . . or is ended. When everything is known, we're at the end of the reel. Ballard often takes the opposite approach, dwelling on the likely possibility that we've already arrived at the end, overloaded with too much (non-)information and no obvious front end on the Multivac to illuminate things. On one hand, information is at its maximum overdrive—aggregational extremity; on the other, the only consolation is found in the minimalist path of computational quietism. Unfriending Mulitvac. In light of WolframAlpha's trillions of elements of computable knowledge, one is tempted to say, We spooled to the end of the *Encyclopedia Galactica* pretty fast, right? And, if "overhead, without any fuss, the stars were going out," as in Clarke's famous story "The 9 Billion Names of God," then don't panic.[53]

53. Arthur C. Clarke, "The Nine Billion Names of God," in *The Other Side of the Sky*, 3–14 (New York: Harcourt Brace, 1958).

Pop Culture Today; or, Plasticman, Where Are You?

NOT LONG AGO, an announcement about a screening of *Metropolis* came across my social media feed. The municipal art museum was sponsoring a summer film series on films that had inspired *Star Wars*. The very first comment someone wrote under the post was as follows: "Hitler's favorite movie . . . I'll pass." It's a strange thing for someone to assert peremptorily that Hitler's favorite movie was *Metropolis*, that it should be avoided for this reason. For one thing, it is not true. That prize goes to—according to Martin Bormann, at least, who recorded this and other tidbits of table chatter from Hitler—*King Kong*.[1] More on Kong later. But, first, where does this pseudo-proposition come from, why does it have so much currency, and what sense can we make sense it? Fritz Lang's expressionist masterpiece, made in 1927, wasn't a Nazi film, after all. Nor was Lang a Nazi.[2] In fact, he fled the Nazis. The *Gleichschaltung* was

1. For a selection, see Adolf Hitler, Norman Cameron, R. H. Stevens, and H. R. Trevor-Roper, *Hitler's Table Talk, 1941–1944: His Private Conversations* (New York: Enigma Books, 2000). For confirmation that Hitler was a fan of *King Kong*, see Ernst Hanfstaengl, *Hitler: The Missing Years* (1957; repr., New York: Arcade, 1994), 221, as well as Volker Koop, *Warum Hitler King Kong liebte, aber den Deutschen Mickey Maus verbot* (Berlin: be.bra, 2015).

2. Leaving aside the complicated issue of possible toxic subtexts in *Metropolis* and their etiology (including the error of calling the director a fascist for representing a [quasi-]fascist dystopia in his film), Lang exited Nazi Germany on July 31, 1933, claiming later that his departure was motivated by an uncomfortable meeting with Reich minister of propaganda Joseph Goebbels, in which Goebbels, Lang claimed, expressed his admiration for his films and tried to draft him to the cause of chief Nazi film propagandist. See Gösta Werner, "Fritz Lang and Goebbels: Myth and Facts," *Film*

47

clearly the cause of his flight. *Gleich* means "the same"; *Schaltung* means something like "circuitry," "wiring," "configuration." Lang wanted no part of the coming reconfiguration of society and culture under the repressive controls and authoritarian idiocies of the Nazis.

The distributive principle—pop cultural connectivity—is what I wish to explore: the meaning of the statement that *Metropolis* was Hitler's favorite movie. It's a sloppy version of Siegfried Kracauer, I suppose—for which the director's actual politics, his particular enmity to Nazis—is irrelevant.[3] The concept of a cultural telephone game makes the pseudo-statement *Metropolis was Hitler's favorite movie* . . . true. Why do people like this mistaken notion? Click, like, the idea, Hitler's favorite movie, is what I mean. Leslie Fiedler's point is something else. Fiedler, the pioneering commentator on popular culture, "unrestructured dilettante," in his words, notes that he too likes *King Kong* and makes what he calls a disconcerting "discovery" about connectivity, the popular, and the aesthetic:

> It not only joins together the poor and the rich, the educated and the uneducated, male and female, children and adults, but the good and bad as well; that in the enjoyment of popular literature one is joined to those people who are felt to be socially reprehensible, wicked, whatever your social code and values may be. Popular literature joins you and your worst enemies as well as your worst self![4]

Quarterly 43, no. 3 (1990): 24–27. It is also worth mentioning that Lang's mother was Jewish. For a discussion of the anecdote, see Tom Gunning, *The Films of Fritz Lang: Allegories of Vision and Modernity* (London: British Film Institute, 2000), 8–11.

3. Kracauer cites Hitler's interest in *Metropolis* specifically—gleaned from another interview with Lang—but the thrust of his argument concerns the role of Weimar cinema in preparing the ground for Nazism, by externalizing "deep psychological dispositions" toward obedience to authoritarian domination through "subterranean content that, like contraband [crosses] the borders of consciousness without being questioned." Siegfried Kracauer, *From Caligari to Hitler: A Psychological History of the German Film* (1947; repr., Princeton, N.J.: Princeton University Press, 2004), 163–64.

4. Leslie Fiedler, *The Devil Gets His Due: The Uncollected Essays of Leslie Fiedler* (Berkeley: Counterpoint, 2008), 22.

The field of consumption is a plane of risky connectivity, a technical interface, a platform for bringing popular things and favorite things together outside the laws of critical intelligence.

What does it mean to call one movie your favorite anyway? Does it mean that you watch it over and over again? That you think other people should watch it this same way on repeat? Or, is it more like the setting of preferences, exteriorizing them, making them conspicuous as yourself to others? That you'd like them to check it out, to test if it could be one of their favorite things, too? That you'll go back to it? Or else, it signals the hazards of consumption—*raindrops on roses and whiskers on kittens*—these things may also be fascist? What-Hitler-likes is an odd metric. Fielder points to the sudden appearance of the popular in the aesthetic, the discovery of significance in the consumption of popular culture in the sense of all things touched by the aesthetic in the collaborative admixture of the monstrous and the trivial. Beware what you like or you may like Adolf Hitler—once described by Theodor Adorno as "a mixture of King Kong and a suburban hairdresser."[5] The colossal reality-warping character of a zone made of, in Jacques Rancière's words, "free and equal individuals . . . dragged together into a ceaseless whirl in search of an excitement that was nothing but the mere internalization of the endless and purposeless agitation of the whole social body."[6] Excitement gives way to connectivity—an unbounded, hypersynchronized infinite distraction, as Dominic Pettman puts it, in which "we never feel the same way as other potential allies and affines at the same moment? [W]hile one person is fuming about economic injustice or climate change denial, another is giggling at a cute cat video."[7] In effect, this platform optimizes distraction as a massified aggregate reception horizon.

5. Qtd. in Stefan Müller-Doohm, *Adorno: A Biography* (Cambridge: Polity, 2005), 182.

6. Jacques Rancière, "Why Emma Bovary Had to Be Killed," *Critical Inquiry* 34, no. 2 (2008): 233–48.

7. Dominic Pettman, *Infinite Distraction* (Cambridge: Polity, 2016), 29.

"Torn from its obviousness in order to become a hieroglyph, a mythological or phantasmagoric figure," "the ordinary becomes beautiful as a trace of the true," Rancière notes in *The Politics of Aesthetics*, describing what we might call pop culture degree zero.[8] Enter King Kong, the "tallest, darkest leading man in Hollywood."[9] Meet the Campbell Soup can: "I used to drink it. I used to have the same lunch every day, for 20 years, I guess, the same thing over and over again."[10] Presto change-o! the Las Vegas Strip becomes the postmodern apotheosis of complexity and contradiction in architecture.[11] The reason *visibility* might be preferred to *legibility* in these references is that the aesthetic is not a discursive field to be read—or interpreted—but a platform to be suddenly seen, accessed, or processed, to be seen looking for exciting objects of attention and affection. The person being somebody is only completed by connections with the kitsch that arrives on her threshold, kitsch that is now given a strictly agnostic valence—as the cultural given, the data. Data ("flows . . . more vast than anything the world has seen," Pynchon writes) seem "jumbled up together" in mixtures of "profane and sacred, uncivilized and cultured, antique and modern, that each sum up a world."[12] Too much data (Online) replace more life (in Lit.). Agency is located not within a single human being per se as a condition of exemplary personhood but gets distributed outside. The emancipation of the zone. Broadcast in and through a newly sensible popular domain, a connected platform—"graffiti, shop signs, or catalogues of out-of-date merchandise" and so forth—it is administered in and as aesthetic-bureaucratic smegma, to recall Tyrone Slothrop's desk

8. Jacques Rancière, *The Politics of Aesthetics* (New York: Bloomsbury, 2013), 52, 30.

9. Pynchon, *Gravity's Rainbow*, 179.

10. Andy Warhol, *I'll Be Your Mirror: The Selected Andy Warhol Interviews*, ed. Kenneth Goldsmith (New York: Carroll and Graf, 2004), 18.

11. Robert Venturi, Steven Izenour, and Denise Scott Brown, *Learning from Las Vegas* (Cambridge, Mass.: MIT Press, 1972).

12. Rancière, *Politics of Aesthetics*, 37.

in Psysection, in the great novel about these themes, Thomas Pynchon's *Gravity's Rainbow*.[13] Blissful ignorance, benighted stupidity, determined prejudice, give way to an animate tissue of dissatisfactions, disruptions, interruptions. In the ruins of Europe, the last months of World War II, Pynchon's anti-hero sits in the wreckage reading a Plasticman comic, gathering more counsel from its pages about how to adapt to this setting than from any of the official briefings from HQ.[14]

From about a century earlier, it is Emma Bovary who provides Rancière's hero as networked aesthetic receiver: "The heroine of a certain aesthetic democracy . . . Bovary wants to bring art into her life, both into her love life and into the décor of her house. The novel is constructed as a constant polemic against a farm girls desire to bring art into life. It contrasts 'art in life' (this will later be called the aestheticization of daily life) with a form of art that is in books and only in books." Bovary's *agon* is the wasteland of freely appropriated total sensibility—"paths of communications opened up in the earth itself" (i.e., popular content wants to be free)—ripe with all kinds of banalities and stupidities. Here the accounting he has in mind is unliterary *pars pro toto*—not merely against "the chatter of newspapers" but also against the nullification of all "fatal words written on paper."[15] Opposing this is what Rancière nominates as "a good form of writing . . . inscribed in things themselves," a "form of writing [that] can only mean, in the end, the self-cancellation of literature." That he calls this ruined condition for Lit. writing is weird, for there are no pure criteria left for inscription—besides the "excitement" of jostling in the

---

13. Rancière, 54.

14. Pynchon, *Gravity's Rainbow,* 206.

15. Rancière, *Politics of Aesthetics,* 54. See Janice Radway, *Reading the Romance: Women, Patriarchy, and Popular Literature* (Chapel Hill: University of North Carolina Press, 1984). On the relation between Bovary's reading habits and popular reading practices around popular romance novels, see Dorothee Birke, *Writing the Reader: Configurations of a Cultural Practice in the English Novel* (Berlin: DeGruyter, 2016).

heterogeneous aesthetic whirlwind. While not necessarily invest-
ed in technicity, Rancière is indeed dreaming of his modernism
without moderns, a dark Kantianism that provides the imaginative preconditions for a total connectivity network of distraction
and interruption: "the sensible framework defined by a network
of meanings, an expression does not find its place in the system
of visible coordinates where it appears. The dream of a suitable
political work of art is in fact the dream of disrupting the relationship between the visible, the sayable, and the thinkable without
having to use the terms of a message as a vehicle."[16]

Instead of a Kantian *sensus communis,* the heroic idea that everyone has access to the same perception of the aesthetic, the sudden
appearance of the popular as an aesthetic platform, entails zones
of attention and inattention, calls forth something different. Enter
Rancière's virtuous dissensus ("being together apart") that I would
propose as something like being distracted together.[17] Dissensus
dismantles of criteria around itself, dissolving the literary into distributed sensibilities ("fusing literature and life and making any
source of excitement equal to any other," he writes) and pricking
itself with various inoculations of ignorance, dissatisfaction, stupidity, distraction, favorites, popularity, readily "incorporated into
anybody's life" and "become part of the scenery and the furnishings
of everyday life."[18] In his response to Alain Badiou's *Handbook of
Inaesthetics,* Rancière points to a modernism without modernism—
the modernist variant described in *Politics of Aesthetics* as the "mode
of sensible being proper to artistic products"—that arrives specially
defined by its necessity for explication from outside—the cultural
thing arrives intertwined, as it were, with the literary-philosophical
operator manuals that provide "orientation[s] for thought." "Such
is the paradox of the aesthetic regime in the arts," he writes. "It
posits the radical autonomy of art, its independence of any ex-

16. Rancière, *Politics of Aesthetics,* 51.
17. Rancière, 54.
18. Rancière, "Why," 240.

ternal rule. But it posits it in the same gesture that abolishes the mimetic closure separating the rationale of fictions from that of facts, the sphere of representation from other spheres of existence." Rancière's pure "aesthetic regime" is made of impure stuff (disrupting the "Romantic quagmire . . . bogged down in the humus of fossils") that might be usefully compared to Arthur Danto's Artworld. Less an autonomous preserve for aesthetic purity, it calls attention to the institutionalized ways of seeing heteronymous ingredients aesthetically that don't get noticed otherwise.[19] "To see something as art," writes Danto, "requires something the eye cannot de[s]cry— an atmosphere of artistic theory, a knowledge of the history of art: an Artworld."[20] Instead of a totaled Berlin, Slothrop envisions a totalized "apescape," inserting uncanny pop cultural references as a multimediated alibi into the ruined literary–historical environment:

> Well, what it is—is? what's "is"?—is that King Kong, or some creature closely allied, squatting down, evidently just, taking a shit, right in the street! and everything! a-and being ignored, by truckload after truckload of Russian enlisted men in pisscutter caps and dazed smiles, grinding right on by—"Hey!" Slothrop wants to shout, "hey lookit that giant *ape*! or whatever it is. You guys? Hey . . ." But he doesn't, luckily. On closer inspection, the crouching monster turns out to be the Reichstag building, shelled out, airbrushed, fire-brushed powdery black on all blastward curves and projections, chalked over its hardechoing carbon insides with Cyrillic initials, and many names of comrades killed in May.[21]

Only King Kong is "Bad and Big enough to take part in transcendent doings," Pynchon writes elsewhere.[22] The precarity of com-

---

19. Arthur Danto, "The Artworld," *Journal of Philosophy* 61, no. 19 (1964), 5710584.

20. Danto.

21. Pynchon, *Gravity's Rainbow*, 368.

22. Pynchon, "Is It Okay to Be a Luddite?," *New York Times*, October 28, 1984, http://www.nytimes.com/books/97/05/18/reviews/pynchon-luddite.html. Referencing a slogan of the 1960s counterculture ("King Kong Died for Our Sins"), Pynchon describes "Kong" as the "classic Luddite saint," the only "countercritter Bad and Big enough" to counteract "what

mon social existence is, in this sense, the animate background
noise of modernity—"not dysfunctional or a 'strange creature' in
the global economy, but rather . . . functionally constitutive."[23] To
detect a human form factor (a husk of humanism) against the technical backdrop of pervasive precarity ("full of tricks," as Pynchon
has it) isn't an additive process—a version of the social-political
life in which everyone gets ceremoniously counted together.[24]
Rather, it means subtracting a form of aesthetic signal detection
from already damaged conditions available in popular culture.

The background is foregrounding itself.

Those who may or may not be working—the global pool of
the "precarious"—make precarity a perversely privileged position, that is, an opportunity and also "a determinable condition."
Beyond its role as a would-be "identificatory emblem," precarity
operates as its own ambivalent theme. It is the stranger at the door
of the denizen who is enjoined endlessly to prepare for its arrival.[25] Opportunity knocks. Approaching precarity is experienced as
a kind of aesthetic address—critical positioning and aesthetic risk
taking—as much as anything else. A point about the functionality
of these words as risky criteria: the precarity of criteria signals a
vortex of ambivalence that isn't so much about shoring up would-
be identities—not least, aggregate identities—as it heralds something like the arrival of modernity as an inhuman format for dividing individuals into individual units of apprehension and further

---

would happen in a nuclear war." The implication is that even Kong as
the anxious and "irresponsible" apotheosis of "our" toxified pop cultural
coprophelia can't expiate "us" from the death cult of the military–industrial
war machine.

23. Martin Bak Jørgensen, "The Precariat Strikes Back: Precarity
Struggles in Practice," in *Politics of Precarity: Migrant Conditions, Struggles
and Experiences*, ed. Carl-Ulrik Schierup and Martin Bak Jørgensen
(Amsterdam: Brill, 2016), 55.

24. Pynchon, "Is It Okay to Be a Luddite?"

25. Philip Armstrong, "Precarity/Abandonment," in *Nancy and the
Political*, ed. Sanja Dejanovic, 245–71 (Edinburgh: Edinburgh University
Press, 2015).

dividing these into derivative risk positions. Vilém Flusser puts it this way: "One has to possess criteria—the units of measurements and rules—to be able to critique: the yardstick that one applies to the thing one critiques, to judge and decide over it. The tradition knows three kinds of measurement standards: the epistemological ('true-false'), the ethical ('good-bad'), and the aesthetic ('beautiful-ugly')."[26] Just now, criticism about the epistemological, the ethical, and the aesthetic is the ultimate contingent labor nobody wants.

At a distance—from outer space, as it were—pop cultural precarity is the ruined condition for criteria, and risk is the hidden calculation that includes all standards by excluding judgment about the true, the good, and the beautiful from a present situation. It is this calculation about the format of criteria in modernity that is rarely mentioned by name, either positively or negatively. Lately, the known forms of criticism seem precariously confined to precipitously shrinking surfaces. Professions of critical humility abound; commonsensical, descriptive lessons about realism, flat ontologies, the mortifications of theory, denunciations of the folly of hermeneutics, and so on, are legion. What we need now, we're told, is to get back in queue behind the more empirically sensitive/ vulnerable denizens in front of us, attend only to what is readily "evident, perceptible, apprehensible [to them] . . . what insists on being looked at rather than what we must train ourselves to see through."[27] The face of the denizen is itself a precarious surface, a surface that provokes surface reading as surely as any text. What's on the face, like what's in the text, seems to solicit a desire for nothing more than imprecations of epistemological modesty, for confirmations about the value of spending all our time with bogus realism. It's all right there on the face of it. Nevertheless, the surface is inscrutable; it also wants to be read as something else: a screen, a search engine bar. What I have in mind is that we must face up to criticism at the present time, to what Alexander Galloway calls an interface effect: the interface, he writes, is an "agitation" or generative friction between different precarious formats, a "fertile nexus between insides and outsides," across scales, sizes, membranes, and platforms. Criticism might be conceived as an attempt to work through the unworkably precarious criteria of popular culture.[28]

In "Notes on Deconstructing the Popular," Stuart Hall observes that popular culture is a "pretty horrendous" category.[29] Each word—*popular* and *culture*—presents distinct conceptual difficulties, further complicated by joining them together. Chief among these shared difficulties is periodizing the conjunction, imagining life before popular culture, as it were, as a Skull Island fossil of an age before *popular* and *culture* were considered praiseworthy or even key critical concepts. They both promise massive inclusivity without conditions. The pleonastic aspect is striking—*popular culture*—as if underscoring that much of what gets called *culture* isn't particularly *popular* and much of what's *popular* isn't especially valued or visible as *culture* per se. The adjective *popular* comes from the Latin *popularis*, meaning "belonging to the people"—not surprisingly, *populus* means "people."[30] Part of what's at issue here is the question of *to whom culture properly belongs*. Popular culture, possessed and prepossessed by its consumers, foregrounds problems of property and propriety. *Voxpop*—to borrow a word from Meaghan Morris—is the voice of the pop cultural dispossessed (disposed by the functionaries and the admin-

28. Alexander Galloway, *The Interface Effect* (Malden, Mass.: Polity, 2012), 52.

29. Stuart Hall, "Notes on Deconstructing the Popular," in *Cultural Theory and Popular Culture: A Reader*, ed. John Storey (London: Pearson, 1998), 442.

30. *Oxford English Dictionary*, s.v. "popular."

cult of spokespersonship).[31] The sense of the word *popular* being "suited to ordinary people" comes from the late sixteenth century, and it retains a sense of aristocratic disapprobation. What is "popular" is "well-liked [or] admired by the people," and the particular association with ostensibly inconsequential arts and entertainment, in the sense of a "popular song," for example, was already well established in the nineteenth century.[32]

Insofar as popularity becomes associated with new democratic virtues, new audience formations, cultural pluralism, and so forth, it also indexes inflationary dangers in this (quasi-)capitalist system, not least in a democracy of goods in which the price of good goods is correlated with their scarcity. Critical ambivalences such as these are baked in—into the concept of popular culture itself, that is—as Hall explains: a given popular cultural object is coded with "struggle and resistance—but also, of course, appropriation and ex-propriation."[33] Too often, popular culture entails the "active destruction of particular ways of life," as he puts it.[34] The colloquialism *pop* culture—that somewhat archaic abbreviation—gets at this capacity: pop culture *pops*. It has a special capacity to arrest, to shock, to surprise, to zing. Here I'm thinking of Rancière's point about the sudden visibility of "Emma Bovary" as an exemplary cultural consumer, and the threatening meaning that Flaubert ascribes to it. In other words, pop culture designates an approach, an aesthetic instantiated in a sentimental education about things as objects of affection. It is, following Morris, drawing on Michel de Certeau, "a way of operating—rather than as a set of contents, a marketing category, a reflected expression of social position, or even a 'terrain' of struggle."[35]

31. Meaghan Morris, "Banality in Cultural Studies," in *Logics of Television: Essays in Cultural Criticism,* ed. Patricia Mellencamp (Bloomington: Indiana University Press, 1990), 22.

32. *Oxford English Dictionary.*

33. Hall, "Notes on Deconstructing the Popular," 442.

34. Hall, 443.

35. Morris, "Banality in Cultural Studies," 30.

In *Heart of Darkness,* Marlow stumbling around the Congo Free State happens upon "an extraordinary find," a single, discarded book about seamanship near "a heap of rubbish reposed in a dark corner" of an abandoned hut. What arrests him most about his discovery is that someone has annotated it in code: "Yes, it looked like cipher. Fancy a man lugging with him a book of that description into this nowhere and studying it—and making notes—in cipher at that! It was an extravagant mystery."[36] Marlow is astounded to discover a literary artifact of modernity in this context, a critical annotation, evidence of someone's attempt to sort useful information from useless noise (thinking of seamanship, *cybernetics* comes from the Greek word for "helmsman"). Here Marlow is an improbable modernist reader looking for something different to read, except Conrad has created a fictional world where something different to read is also something to read at all. It is a scene of reading in a forensic sense, a reader reconstructing an imaginary scene of another reader before a book. In the anonymous, sedulous reader—the ciphering note taker—he has found a secret sharer. One of the most difficult things of Conrad's novella is coming to terms with Marlow's irresistible need to flatter, adulate, stroke, and tickle this indecent document—not least in this scene, when a reader would be forgiven for assenting to its suppression. Slothrop, reading his Plasticman comic, gives us a related scene—in this version, cybernetic notation no longer hides from view; pop culture comes into the open as a tool of thought charting a way out of the lettered world and into the universe of technical images and Ben-Day dots: "Four-color Plasticman goes oozing out of a keyhole, around a corner and up through piping that leads to a sink in the mad Nazi scientist's lab, out of whose faucet Plas's head now, blank carapaced eyes and un-plastic jaw, is just emerging."[37] Later, Pynchon makes clear that this is also a path into distributed paranoia, "nothing less than the onset, the leading

36. Joseph Conrad, *Heart of Darkness* (New York: Dover, 1990), 34.
37. Pynchon, *Gravity's Rainbow,* 206.

edge, of the discovery that everything is connected, everything in
the Creation, a secondary illumination—not yet blindingly One, but
at least connected."[38]

To some extent, the critical conception of pop culture at work
here is a creature of very recent provenance, sustained by forms of
academic attention and zones of interest associated with cultural studies. Nevertheless, it is worth noting not only that popular
culture exists well before its recent academic invention but also
that it exists as an event that forms critical reflexivity. As countless
commentators have observed, Rancière included, votes and fac-
tories were decisive factors for making *popular* and *culture* mutually articulated concepts. Dennis R. Hall shows that Dr. Johnson
in the mid-seventeenth century, for example, "seriously poses a
question [that is still] common in popular culture studies: 'do the
producers of popular culture create a taste in their audience or do
they respond to a taste already existing in their audience?' Surely,
each modifies the other."[39] Enthusiastically writing for a "popu-
lous" literary marketplace becomes for Dr. Johnson an exercise in
connecting "the ridiculous" and "the profound."[40] As pop culture
collapses the cultural producer and the cultural consumer, it also
blurs differences between pop cultural fandom and aesthetic-
critical environment.[41] Popular culture flickers into self-reflexivity
much like Molière's bourgeois gentleman who discovers he's been
speaking prose all along. The sense that much of pop culture is
readily available for second-order administration is at the center
of its legitimacy struggles for visibility and prestige (as well as a
continuous parade of pop cultural adepts). Patrick Brantlinger

38. Pynchon, 703.

39. Dennis Hall, "Signs of Life in the Eighteenth Century: Dr. Johnson
and the Invention of Popular Culture," *Kentucky Philological Review* 19
(2005): 14–15. Incidentally, Hall sees Donald Duck, not King Kong, as the
pop culture egregore par excellence of the twentieth century.

40. Compare Morris, "Banality in Cultural Studies," 40.

41. For a paradigmatic example, see Radway, *Reading the Romance*,
221.

and James Naremore include Popular in their heuristic of six coarticulated artistic "cultures" in modernity: High, Modernism, Avant-garde, Folk, Mass, and Popular.[42] In their taxonomy, each culture presents a durable disposition emphasizing different constellations of production, consumption, meaning, sensibility, and reflexivity.[43] As an alibi for redeeming Mass with Folk, the Popular resituates Modernism, Avant-garde, and Folk with risk positions and risky ambitions, and so on. It's important to note that forms of connectivity—indeed, plasticity—popular or otherwise, stretch across all dispositions. Indeed, in the formulation, these are not discrete, graduated domains one might be led to suspect but "an unsettled mixture": "if they are real, they partake of one another, sometimes overlapping, blurring together or speaking dialogically—and sometimes, like figures on a chessboard, living in antagonistic relation."[44]

Unsettled and unsettling, the Pop Culture game (more Trivial Pursuit than 3D chess) has been up for "serious" scrutiny for a long time. Instead of the seven classic arts—Architecture, Sculpture, Painting, Music, Poetry, Dance, Performing—in 1924, Gilbert Seldes proposes a taxonomy of seven "lively" arts—comics, movies, musicals, vaudeville, radio, popular music, dance—as all "worthy of a second look."[45] With cultural studies, the heat lamps of reflexive secondary illumination warm a heteronomous variety of phenomena, happenings, scenes, and practices: advertising, fashion, leisure, entertainment, celebrity, music, sports, fashion, gaming, public intellectuals, zines, superheroes, shopping, cosplay, collecting, stand-up, hipsters, guerilla gardening, nerds, King Kong cultism, television, video games, sitcoms, reality TV, cocktail culture, slang, pulp, cult, memes. Recognizing the co-emergence of criticality in

---

42. Brantlinger and Naremore, *Modernity as Mass Culture* (Bloomington: Indiana University Press, 1991), 8–13.
43. Brantlinger and Naremore.
44. Brantlinger and Naremore, 8.
45. Gilbert Seldes, *The 7 Lively Arts* (New York: Dover, 2001).

pop cultural connectivity is crucial. Good pop culture research can't stand apart—or wholly apart—from the objects of its study, nor can it legitimately condescend to them (sweetening lesson plans with homiletic spoonfuls of *The Simpsons* or *Star Wars*), because it is *in the mix*. It is in the mix not just in what pop culture artifacts mean in terms of textual dynamics—coding and decoding signs, for instance—but also in how they work as signals and how they matter in different situations, contexts, and environments. Ideally, attention to meaning and mattering expands hermeneutics to the actual forces and flows of value, information, tech, feeling, power. Putting emphasis on the particular rather than the general, this kind of activity explores the idiosyncrasies of specific audience structures and the emergence of the aesthetic objects and cult artifacts that define them. Working through issues of production as well as consumption, mashing up academic and nonacademic ways of thinking into novel configurations of thought and gesture, pop culture might be best understood as a laboratory of cultural methodology.[46] Making matter matter is a strategically important element of an approach that pays attention to the extended thing, with all the immanent or prognostic powers adduced, *res extensa,* from assorted pop cultural things, fossils, totems, talismans, findings, commodities, jokers, novelties, and trash.[47]

In a bad way, Dwight MacDonald's most popular essay, "Masscult and Midcult," illustrates the workings of the critical legitimacy crisis I have in mind.[48] "The recent [1958] centenaries of Poe and Melville passed without undue excitement in the press," he writes, "but *Sports Illustrated* devoted four pages to the fiftieth

46. See esp. Steven Connor, "Cultural Phenomenology, CP: or, A Few Don'ts by a Cultural Phenomenologist," *parallax* 5, no. 2 (1999): 17–31.

47. This list borrows from the taxonomy proposed by Joshua Glenn and Rob Walker, http://significantobjects.com/. See also Aaron Jaffe, *The Way Things Go* (Minneapolis: University of Minnesota Press, 2014).

48. Dwight MacDonald, "Masscult and Midcult," in *Against the American Grain: Essays on the Effects of Mass Culture,* 3–75 (New York: Random House, 1962).

anniversary of Fred ('Bonehead') Merkle's failure to touch second base in a World Series game" (65).[49] MacDonald is concerned that the Press (Midcult) is more exercised about Sports (the epitome of Masscult) than Literature (the epigone of High Culture). Today, outside rarified circles of the baseball antiquarian, Bonehead Merkel is an all but forgotten footnote, while Poe and Melville remain famous. People honor their birthplaces and graves, read from their works, read translations, watch adaptations, consume product tie-ins and assorted merchandise. The audience for Bonehead Merkle's notorious base-running error were the spectators in attendance at a late-season game in a tight pennant race in 1908 as well as those reading about it in the *New York Times,* in which Merkel was mercilessly scapegoated (*apescaped,* as Pynchon would have it). The controversy surrounding the irregular umpiring of the incident may have led the commissioner of baseball to commit suicide, some speculate, and Merkle never could escape his unjust association with it. Many fans of the New York Giants held Bonehead Merkel responsible for spoiling the team's season. Some fans of the Chicago Cubs took Merkel's Boner as the totemic cause of the Cubs' legendary curses. Deep unpopularity is itself a sign of popularity. *Is it better to be somebody than it is to be nobody or anybody?* to paraphrase Terry Malloy in *On the Waterfront.* Bonehead Merkel provides a real-life, ready-made parable of unpopular pop culture—modern notoriety—as a failure to touch base. No eyewitnesses survive. For almost everybody now, Bonehead Merkel is a nobody. Lit. posterity may or may not be more difficult to achieve than other forms of fame, but once achieved, it is more durable. This, for MacDonald, isn't the issue (though it may be too soon for him to tell about Merkel's "Boner"); the problem is that Midcult always hits its mark: "a tepid ooze . . . spreading everywhere."[50]

49. MacDonald, 65.
50. MacDonald, 54.

Again, the issue is that the popular implies connectivity understood as anonymous and heteronomous touching:

> the danger to High Culture is not so much from Masscult [writes
> MacDonald] as from a peculiar hybrid bred from the latter's unnatural
> intercourse with the former. A whole middle culture has come into
> existence and it threatens to absorb both its parents. This intermediate
> form—let us call it Midcult—has the essential qualities of Masscult—
> the formula, the built-in reaction, the lack of any standard except
> popularity—but it decently covers them with a cultural figleaf. In
> Masscult the trick is plain—to please the crowd by any means. But
> Midcult has it both ways: it pretends to respect the standards of High
> Culture while in fact it waters them down and vulgarizes them.[51]

Displaced anxieties about "unnatural intercourse" aside, the essay
resembles nothing less than a Midcult version of Adorno—*the ene-
my within* being administrative functionary whose self-appointed
task is to report upon "what-the-public-wants," and the voxpop
ventriloquism confuses evaluation, measurement, and management at every turn (either by applause meter or by collecting
"1,036 pages of data and interpretations without offending any
religious, racial, political or social group").[52] Measurement facil-
itates domination; value gets attributed in the rearview mirror. In
a zone where pop culture retrofits "value" to popularity, Plas and
Anton Webern are equally obscure (either reference presupposes
a high level of erudition); MacDonald's essay is symptomatic of the
very hegemony of hybrid and heteronomy he wishes to avert. In
the universe of pop cultural annotation, Bonehead Merkle shakes
hands with Herman Melville and Edgar Allan Poe right here before your eyes as MacDonald makes the introductions.

Let's end this foray into pop culture notation as a form of
critical thought in the animate ooze of a televised debate from
the 1980s (on *Nightline*) about the merits of the latest cinematic
box-office juggernaut in the Star Wars franchise, a video artifact

51. MacDonald, 37.
52. MacDonald, 54.

of which someone uploaded online as a relic of the rapidly fading past.[53] The anonymous comments section, that pop cultural trash compactor at the end of history, alternates between those scandalized by pop cultural sacrilege (who belittles Star Wars?) to those lamenting the loss of high-minded critical civility from our primetime national discourse to those who marvel at the astute judgments by the loyal pop cultural opposition combating kitsch in space. With the much anticipated third installment of a trilogy mere days away, the debate itself consists of a mild give-and-take between three men, a tandem of sweater-wearing movie critics (the "Sweater Guys"), with their own television show and newspaper columns, proudly proclaiming allegiance to the popular, on one hand, and a solitary film and drama critic of a starchier bent, who writes for serious papers and newsweeklies, on the other, and is deeply hostile to the popular. (It should be noted that these three discussants are not academics in any sense.)

The host gets at things quickly: *was the original Star Wars good or bad*? he pointedly asks. And later, to the heart of things: *okay, but, is it great cinema?* The site of struggle over critical frontiers of the Good, the Bad, and the Great—conflict over the Popular—comes down to marking out particular zones for a virtuous affective response concerning the aesthetic, marking out relations to audience enthusiasm, in particular. Right out of the gate, the hostile critic (dubbed "Mr. Grouchy McHighbrow" by one commenter) plays pop cultural kill-joy, a villain who dares to disparage a much-loved cultural object as "malodorous offal," deriding the cultlike response it stimulates. His aversion, he says, is directly proportional to the wild responses of fans as well as the (Masscult) critics who emulate them: "the raves [are] so violent and extravagant one cannot afford to mince one's words if one dislikes these things." For him, the films are bad because they "dehumanize" au-

---

53. "Siskel and Ebert Defend Star Wars," https://www.youtube.com /watch?v=Ky9-eIlHzAE.

diences, and fans and critics alike are subject to their ploys. The word *dehumanize* is significant not least because it really means *infantilize*. *Think of the children*—as Helen Lovejoy would have it on *The Simpsons*. Children, from this vantage, are either subjects for uplift into fully enlightened human adulthood or potential victims for dehumanization through aesthetic desensitization: "Let's face it," he says, Star Wars movies "are for children or for childish adults. They are not for adult mentalities, which unfortunately means that they are not for a lot of my fellow critics who also lack adult mentalities." The first of the two pop cultural enthusiast critics says he "totally disagrees." The disagreement is not premised on any stated position but on an inferred relation between acclaim (even among children) and cultural value. In other words, to dislike Star Wars is to dislike children, insinuates Sweater Guy #1, recalling a childhood spent watching "serials and Saturday matinees" and having his "imagination stimulated." Star Wars is virtuous because it helps you stay "young at heart." In truth, he basically presents another version of Lovejoy's *think of the children* reaction. Children are people, too! Sweater Guy #2, his partner, backs him up by describing a viewing in a movie theater full of rapt and "ecstatic" children whose imaginative hyperdrive was fully operational by the administration of moral value (in "asking each other who's who," "rooting for the right guys, booing the bad guys," etc.).

Both sides, it must be noted, have remarkably little to say about the film itself (or "the normal standards by which we judge movies is this a great film," as the host puts it), despite arguing about the merits of special effects ("when you have a film that's ninety percent special effects, you might as well be watching an animated cartoon," according to Starchy McHighbrow). Yet, the idea of critical reflexivity as a gateway to the rare air of high cultural prestige, however old-fashioned, is anything but defunct. Both sides of the Star Wars debate eagerly play the part of gatekeepers to the human zoo—what George Yúdice has described as culture-as-resource—as a pseudo-place that simultaneously legitimizes, preserves, and enshrines the durable value of popular enthusiasms as an exploitable standing reserve.[54] Once upon a time, this site might have been a debate about Star Wars on *Nightline*; now it happens with every reposted listicle on social media. Even though the Sweater Guys don't self-consciously position themselves as cultural gatekeepers in this venue—mere spokespeople for what's popular, whatever hits its mark—their oft performed role of Masscult apologists trades on the bread and butter of respectable Midcult administration.

The laboratory upstairs is brightly lit, well ordered, crammed with blown glass, work tables, lights of many colors, speckled boxes, green folders—a mad Nazi scientist lab! Plasticman, where are you?[55]

54. George Yúdice, *The Expediency of Culture: Uses of Culture in the Global Era* (Durham, N.C.: Duke University Press, 2003). My reading of Yúdice is influenced by Francis Mulhern, *Culture/Metaculture* (New York: Routledge, 2000), and Peter Osborne, "'Whoever Speaks of Culture Speaks of Administration as Well': Disputing Pragmatism in Cultural Studies," *Cultural Studies* 20, no. 1 (2006): 33–47.

55. Pynchon, *Gravity's Rainbow,* 314.

Imipolex *S/Z*

The Imipolex question was planted for him by somebody, back at the Casino Hermann Goering, with hopes it would flower into a full Imipolectique with its own potency in the Zone.

—THOMAS PYNCHON, *Gravity's Rainbow*

Man becomes, as it were, the sex organs of the machine world, as the bee of the plant world, enabling it to fecundate and to evolve ever new forms. The machine world reciprocates man's love by expediting his wishes and desires, namely, in providing him with wealth.

—MARSHALL MCLUHAN, *Understanding Media*

THE STATUS of Pynchon's masterpiece *Gravity's Rainbow* as an epitome of postmodernism is well established. "If Thomas Pynchon didn't already exist in secrecy, he would have to be invented in order to verify postmodernism," writes Kittler.[1] Insofar as we should now ironize postmodern indeterminacy, the impulse follows from features Kittler spotlights here, the Pynchonian sense that verification is preprogrammed remotely by fabrications and functionaries. Against the new realist uncriticality, Pynchon might help us investigate a durable literary–historical interface between epistemological confidence and ontological confusion that may have been baked into media modernity all along. This

1. Friedrich Kittler, "Pynchon and Electro-Mysticism," *Pynchon Notes* 54–55 (2008): 108–21.

chapter looks at the hidden phenomenology of technical images of alternative modernity in Spoilers, Triggers, Black Boxes. I'm not only interested in discussing what Kittler calls "electomystical" currents but also in situating Pynchonian modernism in an expanded account of meaning of material in inhumanist modernity. This modernity depends on the disruptions of cause/effect facilitated by the technical image, the dark phenomenology of programs, and the real abstractions of hidden metadata. Compressed into black boxes and conditioned by Imipolex G—the spoiler becomes the trigger, reorienting modernity to a hidden administrative program of the apparatus, operating like the camera shutter release or a V2 rocket launch protocol, transforming signs into signals and communications into risk calculations. Beyond the zero is the Golem of inhuman automatization, a style of management as more metadata—more potential indexes—that's smaller, less graspable, and more controlled.

Imipolex G. Spoiler alert: I'm going to tell you all about it. "The material of the future," it's at once a Nazi polymer and a MacGuffin that's linked somehow—by time-based proximity—to the central hermeneutic enigma of *Gravity's Rainbow*. Imipolex G was used to condition the erections of Tyrone Slothrop—you may or may not already know this: he's the pseudo-protagonist of Pynchon's meganovel—so as to anticipate, guide, and perhaps even remotely trigger the ballistic trajectory of Nazi rockets. Eventually (right before the end of the book, that is), someone else—not Slothrop, who's still MIA—but another person, will get encapsulated in Imipolex, blackboxed in the nose-cone compartment of Rocket 00000, erected on the V-2 launch pad, and then rocket-launched. Like Schrodinger's cat, for a given observer, the body hovers in-form, in a suspended state between input and output, simultaneously alive and dead, between remote detonation and telematic control, as if to herald one of the new weapons of control Gilles Deleuze foretells in his famous postscript: the human body becoming form factor for data throughput, becoming technical, recording hidden information for invisible ledgers. The spoiler is the ontically indeterminate given.

It's all here: the spoiler, the trigger, the black box, bio-imipolectique ready made for the postontological Zone. The nested file structure is the human form plasticized in a rocket enclosure.

In his *S/Z*—his decantation of Balzac's novella *Sarrasine* into what he calls 561 lexia, 561 miniaturized units of rereading—Barthes insists that the program runs on "homeopathic rhythm."[2] This homeopathic rhythm—the minute microdose of harm that triggers a critical immune response—alternates between witnessing and forgetting: "Forgetting meanings is not a matter for excuses, an unfortunate defect in performance; it is an affirmative value, a way of asserting the irresponsibility of the text, the pluralism of systems (if I closed their list, I would inevitably reconstitute a singular, theological meaning): it is precisely because I forget that I read."[3] The recognition that *all that is* has already happened is "significant data," means that the conditions are already in-formed for processing. It's programmed, in other words, and, as such, the world of textuality is a kind of shipping manifest of spoilers; the "galaxy of signifiers" present themselves as a reflexively and informationally securitized universe.[4] Barthes's recipe is, in effect, to pasteurize—which is not to say homogenize—to prevent spoiling from mattering.

Thinking of time spent reading *S/Z*, perhaps, Boris Groys writes that "the pleasure of textuality" works like "a nice vacation experience": "for along with the subject, every imminent danger—and thus any ontological inquietude—vanishes as well. [It] is a benevolent sea where no sharks lurk, no storms need be anticipated, no underwater rocks obstruct the path, and the water temperature remains constant."[5] Notionally, it might be more accurate to imagine a deep where all the sharks are tagged and counted, skies where all the

2. Roland Barthes, *S/Z* (New York: Hill and Wang, 1974), 23.
3. Barthes.
4. Barthes, 5.
5. Boris Groys, *Under Suspicion* (New York: Columbia University Press, 2012), 28: "The currency in which today's author is being paid is no

weather patterns are already forecast, ocean floors that come with high-def topographical resolution, and so on, and yet nothing physically touched by humans. In short, this understanding of textuality resolves a certain impasse about sequencing signifier/signified by emphasizing new forms of onto-plasticity between background and foreground, what Groys calls "the discourse of flowing sense." The materiality of signs and the signlike markup of everything depend on the hidden topologies of invisible ledgers, hidden databases that "[consider] ordinary things and archival things to be interconnected via a play of differences."[6] In this context, *S/Z* is more than a chestnut of the poststructuralist era. Rather, it marks a place-holder for an epochal shift in the noösphere, all signs becoming plastic, informed as technical triggers for inhuman flows of processing. Authors no longer find their reward in touching attentive readers—Groys says—but in disarming them for unspoiled encounters with ubiquitous signification, visible copies of an invisible god of Big Data. "The data-verse," he writes, "neutralizes every possible rejection by leaving a space for the other, as the saying goes—or, to put it differently, by not annoying potential readers unnecessarily."[7] One does not touch the signifier as much as live inside as its trigger and/or to disarm its effects.

Let's compare Pynchon's own ideas about triggers, programs, and control. Before becoming a novelist, young Pynchon wrote memos for the Boeing corporation concerning the safe handling of missiles: "Good safety practices . . . are redundant," he notes. "You might say one of the objectives of the safety movement . . . is to generate codes from tests, studies of human reactions, statistical data, near misses, everything we can get, to prevent future trage-

---

longer the readers' agreement but their lack of rejection. Today's reader accepts a text not by agreeing with it but only by not considering it personally offensive. The discourse of the flowing sense neutralizes every possible rejection by leaving a space for the other, as the saying goes—or, to put it differently, by not annoying potential readers unnecessarily."

6. Groys, 30.
7. Groys, 28.

dies from ever happening."[8] Every safety protocol is generated—
preceded, in effect—by the accidents it aims to prevent. The acci-
dent occasions the safety protocol—plasticizes it beyond the zero,
to return to Slothrop. What the phrase *beyond the zero* means is
that Pavlovian conditioning eventually transduces the stimulus.
The triggered response anticipates and obviates its own mechanism as safety protocol. First, you set an alarm clock; the alarm
means "wake up"; eventually, you wake up before the alarm. You
are programmed for the clock—the human becoming alarm. It's
alarming. The reader of *S/Z* expects castration, and that's castrat-
ing. The reader of *GR* expects the in-formation of Tyrone Slothrop,
and without his body, someone else has to be produced, substitut-
ed, seconded, as it were. In this case, it's a human body becoming
the technical material of the future.

In addition to a requisite complement of S&M symbolism—
specially selected for the extraordinary occasion by the villainous
Blicero—the sacrificial victim is physically formed into 00000
("made ready for Death") as a technical object ("metal bondage"
in P's phrase). Stuffed inside an Imipolex outfit inside the V-2, the
test subject is plugged in as just another obscure technical component "among the fuel, oxidizer, live-steam lines, thrust frame,
compressed air battery, exhaust bellow, decomposer tanks, and
vents—with one of those valves, the right one, the true clito-
ris, routed directly into the nervous system of the 00000."[9] The
rocket-passenger test subject is duly given a quantum of life support ("vaporized oxygen") to live, a window of heat-resistant
"artificial sapphire" to see, and a "data-link" feeding a one-way
telematic signal from ground control to hear. In a section called
"Hardware," the precise circuitry of this communication system
is left obscure. To convey "multiplexed error corrections" to the
radio guidance system below, all that matters until ballistic apex

8. Pynchon, "Togetherness," *Aerospace Safety* 16, no. 12 (1960): 6–8,
http://www.pynchon.pomona.edu/uncollected/together.html.
   9. Pynchon, *Gravity's Rainbow*, 751.

is the bare life-form, the window to look through, and possibly a remote-controlled hard-on. Humans being the sex organs of machines, indeed. Concerning output, Pynchon makes only this much explicit: "The exact moment of his death will never be known."[10] It is less that the test subject be given a working button to press than that he ends up becoming a button, the very digital switch between life and nonlife. He is technical, empirical, and decisive, as Flusser would say.

Flusser connects this sense of reductio absurdum of the human test subject to making decision automatic—a conjunction of making and letting which he connects to the zero-dimensionality of programs. Ground zero, in effect, is the onto-miniaturization of a finger about to press a button snapping a picture. Here's Flusser, again:

> [Tools] extend their reach further into the natural world and tear objects from it more powerfully and more quickly than the body could do on its own. They simulate the organ they are extended from: An arrow simulates the fingers, a hammer the fist, a pick the toe. They are "empirical." With the Industrial Revolution, however, tools were no longer limited to empirical simulations; they grasped hold of scientific theories: They became "technical." As a result, they became stronger, bigger and more expensive, their works became cheaper and more numerous, and from then on they were called "machines." Is the camera then a machine because it appears to simulate the eye and in the process reaches back to a theory of optics? A "seeing machine"? Ultimately, there is a final decision taken in the act of photography: pressing the shutter release—just like the American President ultimately pressing the red button. In reality, however, these final decisions are only the last of a series of part-decisions resembling grains of sand: in the case of the American President, the final straw that breaks the camel's back: a quantum-decision. As consequently, no decision is really "decisive," but part of a series of clear and distinct quantum-decisions, likewise only a series of photographs can testify to the photographer's intention. For no single photograph is actually decisive; even the "final decision" finds itself reduced to a grain in the photograph.[11]

10. Pynchon.
11. Flusser, *Towards a Philosophy of Photography* (London: Reaktion, 2000), 39.

The verb *to touch* means first a blind contact, in the hope of finding something by chance: a heuristic method in a spoiler.

Let's turn to the famous line from Foucault's conception of biopolitics to try to highlight what I see as the biopolitical implications of the spoiler, or, perhaps, better to say the spoiler implicit in biopolitics: Foucault says in *Society Must Be Defended* "that one of the greatest transformations political right underwent in the nineteenth century was precisely that . . . to take life or let live . . . came to be complemented by a new right which does not erase the old right but which does penetrate it, permeate it. This is the right, or rather precisely the opposite right. It is the *power to 'make' live and 'let' die.* The right of sovereignty was the right to take life or let live. And then this new right is established: the right *to make live and to let die.*"[12] To make live and let die. Highlight a few things about this idea as a hidden program or command line in which control replaces discipline. It represents a glitch in the program of modernity, a substitution with a vital, viral-like character, not replacement per se but complementation, penetration, and permeation—in effect, spoiler as platform. That the near-inversion is a kind of broken chiasmus—a crossing over to unsafety from life to death—is noteworthy. The old right of sovereign power: to take life, let live. A new one: make live, let die. As *taking* turns into *making, letting* suddenly gets a necro- or thanatopolitical spin. The verb form is proposed, in effect, as the horizon of politics. Power and right, the old, disciplinary way; sovereignty and security, the new protocols of control, leave death off the ledger, as it were, but simultaneously weaponize control. Consequently, life is spoiled by its administration. Freedom from administration is an impossible condition.

If the French offers a somewhat different valence, it's only because the sense of spoilage is more acute: *faire vivre et laisser mourir.* Not *take life and let live* but not *live and let live* either. Foucault's formula ironizes laissez-faire—the neoliberal dream of neglect as markets in control. Letting it all go—total flexibility—means subjectivization to, and as, harm and hazard: to be let in, to be allowed inside, that is, is to live, whereas to be left out, outside, is to die. It's not just a matter of space. Time, temporality, and tenses matter here, too. *To let* links etymologically not only to leave behind and to leave out but also to be late and to be last. Those who come last will be left in precarious conditions. I'll try to give biopolitics a more Flusserian spin. Flusser's *Post-History* gives a media-theoretical version of the biopolitical spoiler effect. Roughly speaking, posthistory for Flusser signals the advent of the biopolitical apparatus as a programmed reality. It isn't the End of History in the Fukuyama sense—the end of ideology and triumph of free market liberalism—although there may be something of a shared genealogy between Foucault, Flusser, and Fukuyama. (Spoiler: inherited strains of Nietzsche.) The rise of the algorithms means the end of surprises such as democratic or industrial progress or revolutionary outcomes. Plug in, turn on, tune out is his version of make live and let die. Spoiling the present with the future means that programs have reoriented temporality—the future programming the present. Considering Foucault in this connection, make live is not just about an administrative program for what is living but also takes on the phonemic slippage of live and live, suggesting the oft repeated injunction to "go live." *We're doing it live*! Relatedly, to let die suggests a modern condition where to lift a finger marks the ultimate form of political decision-making. To go live is to hook up to a network of administration—biopolitical life support, in so many words, passports, visas, biometric data: to hook up to a control panel that powers life, securitizes it, makes it safe from risk, adds redundancies. *Let alone* signals neglect as a form of control—to let alone is not to lift a finger. The let die means that humans die without lifting a finger, without others batting an eye, without twitch or gesture: administration of life, consequent death.

In other words:

"Those who seek to substitute their own models for others (for example by shouting 'Hare Krishna') will find such exotic models have been caught by the very models to be substitute," as Flusser writes.[13] For him, posthistory is an algorithm, a trap "to catch the world" by making it informational. Garbage in, garbage out, the human is bracketed inside. This brings to mind a nugget from Tim Morton's *Ecological Thought* about the hypothetical Tibetan astro*naut*. For Morton, it is clearly an astro-naught—*nihilo ad astra*: "Tibetans [accustomed to high-altitude existence] would make the best space pilots," he muses, "especially on long space missions. They would need to learn to operate the equipment. Tibetan culture is all about space. All kinds of images entice us to think big. One image of enlightened mind is that it's like space." Morton's Blicero-like disregard for the Tibetan stranger caught up in a space program is notable. Thinking thinks big—ecologically, that is—by launching the valuable other beyond the zero into the void: "When we think of indigenous cultures," he writes, "we tend to impose a Western ideology of localism and 'small is beautiful' onto them. In the case of at least one culture—nomadic Tibetans—this is a big mistake. Should we wish to send astronauts to Mars, we could do worse than train Tibetans and other indigenous people for the ride. They would only have to learn to push a few buttons. The very people we think of as small may think the biggest of all." This notwithstanding, the idea of the Tibetan astronaut pushing a button, executing a command line, is worth pausing over.

Thinking big and thinking small are really two sides of the same switch for the media-theoretical account of a biopolitical program I'm describing. We might think of it as inhuman acting at scale. For Flusser, miniaturization is as vexed as gigantomachy:

> The defenders of miniaturization [as] alternative technique [he writes] believe that they are fighting the alienating megalomania of apparatus, and that they are returning to human dimensions. If the small action group, the small business, the individual wind-turbine, the ecological vegetable plot, the cooperative family, seem for them

13. Vilém Flusser, *Post-History* (Minneapolis: Univocal/University of Minnesota Press, 2013), 20.

a return to more adequate human proportions, then they are mistaken. The tiny is even less human than the gigantic. The gigantic may be at least "admired," but the tiny disappears from view, it is "worthless." The "small man" and "self-management" are even less human than the "big men" and the multinationals. Never before has man ceased to be the "measure of all things" so radically as with miniaturization. In miniaturization, man becomes a particle, "information data," "bit," or worthless entity.[14]

Programs, he writes, are like tiny "imprints." They no longer come ready loaded with immutable ideals or improvable forms but comprise immaterial formats.[15] The temptation to think thinking without a thinker—or, in Tim Morton's vein, to think a cosmological garden without a cosmological gardener—misses its own epiphenomenal entailment as part of a pernicious shift toward biopolitical programing.[16] Programs themselves take a command that owes nothing to the transcendental or creative genius: "They are the result of [piecework]—minute combinations of 'bits' done by programmers, systems analysts and other similar anonymous functionaries." No divine images or mosaic vision of a cosmos, they function more like ideograms, Flusser writes. Morton's blindspot is that ground control doesn't need indigenous cosmonauts in its capsule. Not as ecological witnesses at least. Taking a page from his conception of ecological thought—the idea of thinking of interconnectedness as a kind of mesh-ware—the biopolitical becomes thinkable when life becomes program, "when scientific interest established itself over animate things (botanics and zoology) [when] it became apparent that animate things may be quantified just like all other things, but that as it was done, something essential escaped through the intervals."[17] The consequent decentering of the human ruins other world-pictures (or models, as VF

14. Flusser, 71.

15. Flusser, 57–59.

16. Timothy Morton, *The Ecological Thought* (Cambridge, Mass.: Harvard University Press, 2012).

17. Flusser, *Post-History*, 47.

calls them) by spoiling the big heroic dimensions of history, such as Virtue, Nature, Reason, and Progress.

Slothrop seeks the information about the rocket he already has: that the rocket informs him, and he informs it, but what the human knows is functionally immaterial. It never matters. The telematic era is a crisis for the functionaries; engineer and surgeon alike become test subjects. Flusser discusses the example of the civic engineer who "knows that the precision with which he calculates the bridge is a problem. And he knows that the bridge will have effects upon the situation that are not quantifiable: aesthetic effects, for instance. He knows that the bridge will change the lives of men. But as a functionary of the road's construction apparatus he does not see himself obliged" to lift a finger for these lives. For our bogus technocratic overlords—the Know-It-Alls, as one recent book names them—research is "not done for the sake of academic curiosity and public betterment but for the creation of successful corporations."[18]

The resonance here is that embodied information for telematic test subjects is strictly inhuman. The proverbial rocket scientist becomes the *non plus ultra* of intelligence, but, as Pynchon shows, the functionary is but "programmed to program," in Flusser's words. The idea of a technical platform for a telematic society— the internet, in so many words—"oscillate[s] between cinema and supermarket."[19] Its space is not ruled by experts but populated by data: "we are all pieces in a game, inside which we oscillate rhythmically." The players of the game become chess pieces (think the Imipolex "white knight, molded out of plastic").[20] When setting up the game, Flusser notes, it makes no difference to distinguish players and pieces: "The transcoding and irradiation of messages

18. Bradley Babendir, "Peter Thiel's Unfortunate World: On "The Know-It-Alls" by Noam Cohen," *Los Angeles Review of Books*, February 11, 2018, https://lareviewofbooks.org/article/peter-thiels-unfortunate-world -on-the-know-it-alls-by-noam-cohen.

19. Flusser, *Post-History*, 61.

20. Pynchon, *Gravity's Rainbow*, 436.

results in the transformation of the original structure: the trees work linearly, the media, multidimensionally. If we admit that linearity is the structure of history [one thing after another], the media present themselves as post-historical communication. They are black boxes that have history as input and post-history as output. They are programmed to transcode history into post-history, events into programs."[21] Connectivity itself, in other words, is black-boxed inside the program. The platform neutralizes events at all scales: holiday traffic jams in the so-called developed world mirror overloaded trucks of monocultural produce on the margins; social mobility mirrors urban gigantism; inexorable advancement of a global south means permanent migrancy. Flusser's account emphasizes what Foucault calls "an explosion of numerous and diverse techniques for achieving the subjugation of bodies and the control of populations."[22] The migrations of populations signal an openness, a functional lassitude about collective death. Migrants occupy not palaces but slums or stateless refugee camps. To be permanently "undergoing development," he notes, is the fate of the defeated, and the long trend of the migration of peoples bends the right to live toward population replacement by the unborn. These future people are more capable of being "defeated faster" and being "better programmed" as precarious outsiders whose own "children [will have barely] managed to survive."[23]

For the functionary, the platform is reality proper. The functionary expects rights—user privileges, in effect—within the program. The vector of signification is inverted: the concrete person, the passport receiver, is the one that signifies the passport. Reality is the passport; the person gives "meaning" to the passport in the codified world. Black-boxed in this apparatus, Flusser writes, Kulturkritik is an anachronism: "Apparatus always functions increasingly independently from their programmer's intentions. And apparatus

21. Flusser, *Post-History,* 54.
22. Foucault, *Society Must Be Defended,* 140.
23. Flusser, *Post-History,* 65.

that are programmed by other apparatus emerge with increasing frequency. Programmers do not own the decisions made automatically." Inside the V-2, "all function according to an inertia inherent to them and such functionality escapes, from a certain point, the control of the initial programmers. In a final analysis such apparatus function, all of them, toward the annihilation of all their functionaries, including their programmers."[24] For Flusser, like Agamben and many others, the zero hour of the Program is Auschwitz: "Apparatus spring, just like mushrooms after a Nazi rain, from the ground that has become rotten," he writes. Auschwitz is the "shipwreck" of all categories, the "revolutionary event" that overthrew "culture with program."[25] Heroic efforts to think big—moonshots, cracking the genomic code, thinking cosmic interconnectivity—only cover up a compulsion to repeat a programmatic turn with alibies that retain its catastrophic form. This is the meaning of *Zwölfkinder*, where Pynchon is anticipating Bansky's Dismaland. The finger is raised, as if touching the end of a divine fuse; the button initiates life, tangling a subject in time, space, matter, and archival traces. The exact moment of information will never be known. The verb *to touch* means first a blind contact, in the hope of finding something by chance: a heuristic method.

24. Flusser, 21.
25. Flusser, 20.

[... After the Media]

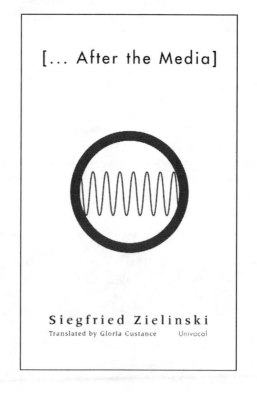

Siegfried Zielinski

Translated by Gloria Custance   Univocal

Conclusion: Updating as Modernity; or, Impermanent Test Dept.

THE LAST SPOILER: after the end come the credits, . . . after the credits, the postcredits. And so on. What follows is an attempt to get there first, to judge a book by its cover at last and annotate the cover of Siegfried Zielinski's [. . . After the Media]—specifically, the English version, the translation, published by Univocal.[1]

A cover per se—a title, an author, an image—but also its tactile qualities call out for annotation. Understood as a paper object, the cover conveys a feeling of hipster technique, flavors of artisanal tattoos, confessions of paper junkies. Theory lingers around as paper elegy. Is theory itself the last rites for paper? Overturning the old cliché about *not judging a book by its cover, [. . . After the Media]* justifies itself in making this thesis visible. With the advent of photomontage, covers acquire new technical abilities, Walter Benjamin claims. The cover itself becomes a political instrument.[2] For a particular book that claims, in an age after the media, that the media is no longer good for politics, is the literary artifact—that old legacy instrument—also no good? Is there still a book, an improbable revenant, that will change your life?

The "archival quality" of its handmade covers picks up dirt as if by design. Or seems to. Rips too easily. The materials are printed, cut, and bound in an atelier, the endpapers note. I watched a YouTube video about it, scored with a track by a band named

1. Siegfried Zielinski, [. . . *After the Media*] (Minneapolis: Univocal/ University of Minnesota Press, 2013).
2. Walter Benjamin, "The Author as Producer," in *The Essential Frankfurt School Reader*, 254–69 (New York: Continuum, 1988).

The Books called "There Is No There." *Scratchy samples* are the rough equivalent of a literary revenant, perhaps. The clip is titled *Letterpress Theory*: "Letterpress printing is a technique of relief printing using a [mechanical] printing press, a process by which many copies are produced by repeated direct impression of an inked, raised surface against sheets or a continuous roll of paper."[3]

> In June 2011, Univocal Publishing was founded by Jason Wagner and Drew Burk as an independent publishing house specializing in artisanal editions and translations of texts spanning the areas of cultural theory, media archeology, continental philosophy, aesthetics, anthropology, and more. [Our] books combine traditional printmaking techniques with the creative evolutions of the digital age and featured letterpress covers designed by publisher and proprietor Jason Wagner, who also provided funding for Univocal.

The idea of humans making their own books, mechanically produced ink-aura[4]—did it ever happen that way? The matter of the bracket of Zielinski's title, the *Klammerzeichen,* a typographical aside, pleonastically reinforces ellipses of tactility. Pause, Pause, Pause. Press, Press, Press. Tap, Tap, Tap.

The media doesn't mediate. It doesn't come in the middle but comes first, then hesitates.

The emblem is a target for a coffee stain. Logo without logos, the cover image represents some kind of oscilloscope, I suppose. A trigger is pressed. A beam of electrons moving across the phosphorescent screen of a cathode ray tube referenced in paper form a time-based circuit, a paleoscreen in which a light pencil moves steadily left to right. A waveform instrument written from a program in which *the coordinate grid has two perpendicular lines, or axes, labeled like number lines, the horizontal x-axis, touch, the vertical y-axis, time. The point where the x-axis and y-axis intersect is the origin of tube attention.* The emblem recalls the instrument that measures oscillating connectivity: "The word [oscilloscope] is an etymological

3. https://en.wikipedia.org/wiki/Letterpress_printing.
4. http://univocalpublishing.com/.

hybrid. The first part derives from the Latin, to swing backwards and forwards; this in turn is from *oscillum,* a little mask of Bacchus hung . . . in vineyards easily moved by wind. The second part comes from . . . *skopein,* to observe, aim at, examine, from which developed the . . . ending *scopium,* which has been used to form names for instruments that enable the eye or ear to make observations."[5] What vanishes is *graphein*—to write and record. The "purpose [is] to spare the living"—a substitute for sacrifice.[6] The custom of hanging oscilla represents an older practice of expiating the final word.

The waveform is an oscillating plot—launch, flash, crash, repeat.

The oscilloscope is not merely an artifact called forth from the crypt but also a weird aesthetic creature emerging from the laboratory, the workshop, the tinkerer's bench, the atelier, the studio. In 1897, Ferdinand Braun invents the o-scope more as physics curiosity than as measuring instrument.[7] Whatever the hidden origins, the technical thing indexes an aesthetic shape for media thinking, a form given not least for remediating future possibilities out of the past and then back to the future. As Wolfgang Ernst writes, oscilloscopic experimenting simultaneously "belongs" to "cultural history (or the 'history of knowledge,' in more Latourean terms)"— leading to television, for instance—and, from their own point of view ("the point of view of the media themselves"), marks a deeply inhuman, "time-invariant event"—"a level of both the artifact and the epistemological *dispositif* . . . indifferent to the historical."[8] The o-scope reveals electromagnetic oscillation itself—amplitude and frequency—the perception of which implies a real hidden dimension for experience and experiment that in turn gets probed, processed, and scoped,

5. Ian Hickman, *Oscilloscopes* (Oxford: Newnes, 2000), 1.

6. *Encyclopædia Britannica* (London: 1910), 20:347.

7. Jon Peddie, *The History of Visual Magic in Computers* (London: Springer, 2013), 292. See Friedrich Kittler, *Optical Media* (London: Polity, 2009), 191–92.

8. https://appliedvirtualitylab.files.wordpress.com/2015/10/ernst _experimenting-with-media-temporality.pdf.

. . . or sonified, in the instance of contemporary media art practices of Carsten Nicolai. Zielinski calls attention to "the embedded implicit knowledge" revealed in Nicolai's *waveform* experiments, the layered "anamnesis" of media thinking, critical temporality updating, overturning itself, out of phase.[9] The oscilloscope stands on the conceptual substrata of a century-old controversy about information and energy, the affordances of photons and electrons as real abstractions that not only turn and return but also get turned over. They oscillate, conceptually speaking. Input a waveform; output a codex—as Nicolai describes it, in so many words, in a suggestive interview:

> *Oscilloscope is the waveform,* but we are also measuring how they are out of phase. It's the device you usually use for mastering, to avoid strong phasing problems for cutting vinyl, for instance. And we are using this device as a creative tool. Recreating what a mastering engineer would say, "fucking hell, how can I avoid that?" And this is a project we started ten years ago, and finally we will publish the book at the end of the year.

Waveform destiny is announced from beyond human perception; the problems of perceiving data are a function of storage matter and the in/formation of physical media.[10]

Turn off the machines. Kittler's last words.[11] In the German, that seemed too good to be true, for Kittler at any rate—"Alle Apparate auschalten"—shut them all off. Stop the life support, stop the recording machines. Last words might come too soon, but online, do they ever come? Even when the life support is switched off, the discourse networks keep recording. J. M. W. Goethe's

9. Panel discussion, transmediale.12 "In/compatible" symposium, February 5, 2012, Haus der Kulturen der Welt, Berlin.

10. https://youtu.be/zCBIKXFrfNA?t=2m34s.

11. Gill Partington, "Friedrich Adolf Kittler, 1943–2011," *Radical Philosophy* 172 (March/April 2012), https://www.radicalphilosophy.com /obituary/friedrich-adolf-kittler-1943-2011. See also https://propagandum .wordpress.com/2012/05/10/gramophone-film-typewriter-by-friedrich -kittler-%EF%BB%BFbook-review.

mehr Licht comes to mind—more light—for Goethe, there can never can be enough. Throw open the shutters! A witness hovers over the death bed trying to bottle your last breath. Inspiration degree expiration. Then, there's Steve Jobs's more recent example. According to his sister, the novelist Mona Simpson, his were "O wow o wow o wow."[12] Isn't it all just power symbology in the end? Toggling the on–off switch; the circle is zero; the line is one. "We all—in the end—die in medias res," she writes for her brother's eulogy, "in the middle of a story. Of many stories." In fact, this total networked fantasy, with its ersatz transcendence and bogus mimesis, belies platitudes about immortality through storytelling. When the machine freezes, you just hold down the power button. "Turn on, tune in, drop out"—that boring drivel—precisely heralds the age that doesn't know what to do with all its media and then pronounces this condition to be awesome. Forget uploading your mind or even the impracticalities of dying on Facebook; in the end, no one cares about your Yelp ratings. Kittler, only disconnect; Goethe, stay illuminated; Jobs, enter sleep mode.

Somewhere from the protracted legitimacy crises of Humanism—H—comes the anxious idea that literary H is weak about Data. This impulse obscures a stupid complicity with the rule of exceptionally fast idiots that forget nothing, as Flusser describes the telematic brain. Technical vocabulary is important, but we don't need to make cars to learn to navigate and negotiate traffic nor to talk about the catastrophe of automobilism. Instead, we need a DH that has critical HD—high definition—resources for orientation in "a world-wide dialogue about the apparatus."[13] Precision for imprecision, as Zielinski reminds us.

Correspondence to reality across the interface is the given, but the noncorrespondence is hard to verify when half of the equation

12. Mona Simpson, "A Sister's Eulogy for Steve Jobs," *New York Times,* October 30, 2011, http://www.nytimes.com/2011/10/30/opinion/mona -simpsons-eulogy-for-steve-jobs.html.

13. Zielinski, *[. . . After the Media]*, 76.

is hidden. The universe of technical images is one of fuzzy cor-relationism between reality and database: the gadget screen isn't a window but something smudgeable that oscillates from magic lantern to camera obscura. Insight is not possible—instead, hid-den protocols of connectivity do the ruling. What requires the most storage space, the biggest file cabinets, in effect, explains nothing; nevertheless these ministries of the small generate flows of trivialities, microaggressions, spoiler alerts. This is our Data Catastrophe. IRL, the HD in DH, might be seen in this untimely impulse to spoil ourselves with metaphoricity and literariness. H as impermanent test department expiates the finitude of thinking from the endlessness of D. It claims the right to off-switch for the cause exhibiting the invisible.

"In a single lifetime we have to learn to exist *online* and be *offline*."

Aaron Jaffe is Frances Cushing Ervin Professor of American Literature at FSU. He has published *Modernism and the Culture of Celebrity, The Way Things Go: An Essay on the Matter of Second Modernism* (Minnesota, 2014), and other work in modern and contemporary literature, media, and theory.